PORTLAND $$$SUPER $SHOPPER

Connie Hofferber   Terry Hofferber

The Writing Works, Inc.
Mercer Island, Washington

Acknowledgments

Many thanks to our mother, Dorothy, who researched the used book stores for this book, and to our father, Merle, for his assistance in areas formerly foreign to the authors.

For our Grandmother Pauline,
who taught us to "waste not,
want not."

Illustrations by Ted M. Olson
Authors' photo by Bob Ellis

Published by The Writing Works, Inc.
        7438 S.E. 40th Street
        Mercer Island, Washington 98040
ISBN: 0-916076-40-7
Library of Congress Number: 80-51868

CONTENTS

INTRODUCTION

INSTEAD of being frustrated by today's inflation and its effective diminishing of our incomes, we decided to investigate ways to buy the things we need for less money, while not compromising the quality.

This book is the result of more than a half-year's research into Portland-area stores, services, programs, and directories which offer the general consumer products of good quality at prices from 10%-90% less than the same or similar product would be listed in a normal retail outlet.

We say "similar product" because in some cases a new definition of quality should be used along with this book. The affluence of our society has convinced many of us that less than perfect goods are not usable – those with broken packaging, dented corners, or slight imperfections. However, small, repairable, or unseen flaws do not detract from the inherent quality of an item in most cases. For instance, is the scratch on the side of a refrigerator, which is marked down ⅓, going to be hidden by the cupboards? Or, does it matter that the packaging on the half-priced bag of dry dog food has been repaired with masking tape? (Making sure, of course, that the bag still weighs close to the advertised weight.)

We encourage you to visit the liquidators, resale shops, and damaged freight outlets listed in the book, using one of the rules we found valuable: "If we had damaged an item ourselves, would we still use it, or would we throw it away?"

No one will shop in all the places included here, but the book offers a chance to find those places which fit into your lifestyle while saving you money. We have also included ideas which might encourage certain lifestyle changes and help bring you even greater savings.

Some of the real bargains to be found do, however, require an investment of time, such as tailoring a "retro" suit, staining an unfinished oak bookcase, packaging spices bought in bulk. But most do-it-yourself projects are easier than you might think, and many of the stores offer advice or help.

It is also true that bargain shopping may initially take more of your time – sample shops often have only one size in an item of clothing; thrift shops and resale stores don't always size their clothing accurately or at all, which means more browsing. However, as you learn how to bargain shop, and find your favorite places to do it, you will be able to save money with little inconvenience. We have listed some hints to help you get started, and would appreciate receiving your good ideas for inclusion in the next edition of the book.

We know, too, that we've missed some good bargain spots in Portland, and since we intend to revise the book from time to time, we encourage you to send us those we might have overlooked in care of our publisher: The Writing Works, Inc., 7438 S.E. 40th Street, Mercer Island, WA 98040.

The book is not an endorsement of any of the stores listed, but is sort of an annotated Yellow Pages, providing a variety of information. We have not been paid for the paragraphs, nor received any gratuities for them, from any of the merchants listed.

Unless you already spend a lot of time bargain hunting, let this book be your guide and starting point towards more satisfying shopping.

HOW TO USE
THE BOOK

WE HAVE arranged the entries in the book in two ways: first by the type of merchandise, concentrating on new, first-quality goods; second by the type of outlet that sells more than one kind of item, those items often recycled, damaged, or surplus but whose useful life is far from over.

The entries are listed alphabetically under specific subheads, with the description of each store only long enough to give necessary information and to describe the store's personality. Every listing includes address, telephone number, and hours. Acceptance of Visa, Master Charge, credit cards, or checks with identification is noted. We have abbreviated shopping center "S/C."

We have also included information as to the accessibility of each store to the physically disabled because more and more people who use wheelchairs are living independently. A "yes" means we found access easy from parking through the door. Otherwise, the type of architectural barrier encountered was noted.

We visited almost every store to judge atmosphere, ease of shopping, and quality of goods. While phone numbers, addresses, and hours were correct when we wrote the book, these may change between our writing and your reading. (We found a number of stores that had gone out of business since the last printing of the Yellow Pages!) Before traveling long distances to shop, it is a good idea to phone and check hours, address, and the availability of items you wish to buy.

In doing the research, we did not rely solely on prices for comparison, since those change almost weekly. Instead, we searched for percentage differences and have listed those for comparison between "discount" and "normal retail."

We have attempted an abbreviated cross reference system and, in many cases, have listed stores in more than one place. The "see" references below the main headings for stores show where else the merchandise may be found. Two indices have been included: one arranged alphabetically by store name, the

7

other listing stores by area of the region, including: North, Northeast, Northwest, Southwest, Southeast, Milwaukie, Oregon City, Gresham, Tigard, Lake Oswego, Hillsboro, and Beaverton.

We have also listed more than one location for stores with branch outlets, but have not checked them for hours or handicapped access. While those may not differ greatly from the main branch, a phone call before visiting would be wise.

We believe that the ultimate in bargain shopping includes taking the bus and leaving the car at home. Tri-Met (the regional transit authority) operates an outstanding transportation system. Check the Yellow Pages for route information, or call 233-3511 for trip planning assistance.

BARGAIN HUNTING HINTS

İF THE BUSINESS of bargain hunting is new for you, you'll undoubtedly be fascinated by the first few places you visit. But before you actually buy an item, it's good to ask yourself two questions: "What's wrong with it?" and, if it is in good shape, "Why can they sell it so cheaply?" The first is fairly easy to answer. You decide how much of your effort and your money, if any, will have to go into making the item as you want it to be. If the answer is acceptable, buy it. You will be forever bragging about the tiny investment and the marvelous acquisition. The second answer can be the result of a number of circumstances.

Real discount merchandise is not simply merchandise of less quality for less money. The variety of ways merchandisers use to offer the buyer a bargain is truly amazing. Definitions of those ways are offered below as a short course in this aspect of capitalism.

Loss Leader: An item purposely priced low, often at a loss to the store, to entice shoppers in for further shopping.

Discontinued, Closeout: Merchandise that is no longer manufactured or stocked. If the item might require replacement parts, inquire as to their availability.

Overstock: Anything in excess of what a wholesaler or retailer wants to carry, often the leftover wholesale stock after retailers' orders have been filled.

Overrun: Again, excess merchandise, but usually the mistake of the manufacturer as to what retailers will purchase.

Surplus: The term is often used indiscriminately by stores, but for our purposes it means the same as "overstock."

Irregular: Merchandise with slight imperfections, often in the color or size.

Second: Merchandise with more noticeable flaws, usually in construction, which should be marked by the seller (but may not be). Careful evaluation of the flaw will determine whether it is worth the discount to you.

Liquidated: When a business goes "out of business," its stock is often sold, by specific lots or in its entirety, to a **liquidator**

for a fraction of its retail value. The liquidator then marks the stock up enough for his profit but still allows the buyer great savings. Liquidators often buy up freight damaged goods, which assures the heterogeneity of their stocks, while others specialize in one sort of merchandise.

Freight Damaged: If a case lot is damaged in shipping, a retail store will often refuse the shipment. However, often the damage is only to the packaging or to the exterior merchandise. The inside may be in perfect condition and bought for a fraction of its original price.

Sample: An item, usually clothing, which has been shown by a manufacturer's representative to retail buyers. It may be slightly soiled, in limited sizes, usually in perfect condition.

Floor Sample: Those items put on display in a store to be looked at and tried out. They may often be scratched, and are always discounted below the packaged goods.

If you insist on personal attention, department store variety in one place, and a chic atmosphere, most of the stores listed in this book won't fit your needs. Liquidators, surplus houses, and factory outlets make much of their profit by keeping overhead low, hiring few salespersons, staying away from the high rent shopping centers, and sometimes by eliminating individual pricing. We find the browsing through racks, shelves, and tables full of good bargains worth the lower-rent ambience.

Most stores have specific days when new merchandise arrives. Finding out those times will get you in when the picking is best. Many stores don't advertise as a way of cutting costs and announce sales and new shipments with a mailing list of their regular customers. Be sure to ask about those things when you find a store you like.

Even though we have listed stores which have year-round bargains, seasonal shopping of normal retail stores and department stores should not be overlooked in your bargain hunting. "Loss leaders" are used heavily by many retail outlets and (if you can discipline yourself not to buy anything except those things which have been discounted) are worth going after. Many stores also hold end-of-month sales which are widely advertised with savings of at least 20%. End-of-season sales offer tremendous bargains, too, although on definitely picked-over merchandise.

The last rule, of course, is that even if you find a bargain in one store, it is worth checking a few others. Comparison shopping is the name of the game.

Appliances

(Also see Catalog Discounters,
Store Outlets, Thrift Shops)

We have avoided used appliance stores because of the difficulty in evaluating quality. We believe the best bargains are found in freight damaged or discontinued models. A nick or a scratch to the exterior can drop the cost considerably while not impairing the operation. Discontinued models are marked down to make room for incoming shipments. The only drawback to these is the questionable availability of spare parts, but how often does one repair a refrigerator rather than buying a new one?

FACTORY CITY — See Building Supplies

GENERAL ELECTRIC SERVICE CENTER

4232 N.E. Sandy Blvd.	**221-5114**
Hours: M-Sat. 9-5:30	**VISA, MC, checks**
Handicapped access: yes	
Other location:	
14305 S.W. Millikan Way, Bvrt.	**646-1176**

If you can fix it yourself, this is the place to get G.E. parts. But better yet, the service center sells "Class E" small appliances for about 20% off retail. "Class E" means that a faulty appliance was returned to the factory and rejuvenated. All warranties apply. Though neither store has many appliances at any one time, we found a food processor, electric clock, two clock radios, steam iron, coffeemaker, and a handmixer.

Arts, Crafts and Hobby Supplies

(Also see Building Materials, Fabrics)

BASKIN ROBBINS — See Kitchen Supplies

DISCOUNT OFFICE SUPPLIES

539 S.E. 39th   231-8118
Hours: M-F 8-5, Sat. 10-2   VISA, MC
Handicapped access: yes

Slightly outside the downtown business district, but on main bus lines, this well-stocked and organized purveyor of office supplies, art supplies and office furniture sells its inventory at a minimum of 15% off the list prices found in most retail office supply stores. They can do this, they say, because of the large volume of business they do, and because of the no-frills, slightly warehouse atmosphere of their store.

Office supplies from liquid paper to staplers to calendars are sold, as is office furniture from desks, file cabinets, and tables to lamps and wastebaskets. Back-to-school supplies are a good buy, and some merchandise was even less than advertised sales elsewhere.

The FOB cash-and-carry price on furniture is $10 less than if they deliver.

FREEBIE EXCHANGE

1087 S.E. 7th, West Linn   657-4410
Hours: M-F 9-5, 9-9 first Wed. of each month
Handicapped access: curb

The Clackamas County Children's Commission gleans discarded items from citizens, businesses and industry which can be used for myriad arts and crafts projects. Cardboard, fabric scraps, plastics, wallpaper books, milk and egg cartons, ribbon, string, wood and tile scraps are all accumulated and distributed

free to everyone and anyone. When you come to search, bring a
few of your own discards to add to the piles.

STANDARD BRANDS PAINT CO.—See Building Materials

U-Frame-It Shops

Having a print or painting professionally framed with several
colored mats, glass, and a wooden frame can often double the
cost of the artwork. However, trying to cut mats, glue and nail
wooden strips, and find glass to fit a frame is almost impossible
for the amateur at home. U-frame-it shops provide the expertise, the materials, and most importantly, the tools that make
all hard jobs much easier.

We haven't used all the shops, but we have framed many pictures and posters at a couple of them. From friends' reports,
they all give about the same service and are priced competitively.

Stretcher bars for needlepoint canvases and heavy backings
for posters are available, as well as a large selection of mats in
various colors and textures. Frames range from ready-made to
the thin, metal type (which look great around posters) to the
elaborately-carved wooden ones for oil paintings. You nail the
frame together, clean the glass, and assemble the pieces. They
cut the glass, mat, and frame, and guide you on all the other
steps.

BEARD'S FRAME SHOPPES

3001 S.W. Cedar Hills, Blvd., Bvrt.   **643-3051**
Hours: M-F 10-9, Sat. 10-6, Sun. 12-5   VISA, MC, checks
Handicapped access: curb
Other locations:
See the Yellow Pages—Picture Frames-Dealers

THE BLACK KNIGHT

7015 S.E. Milwaukie   **236-9293**
Hours: M-F 9-6, Sat. 10-5   VISA, MC, checks
Handicapped access: yes

CHRISMAN'S FRAME IT YOURSELF

4711 S.W. Beaverton-Hillsdale Hwy.	245-7401
Hours: M-Sat. 10-5; Th, 10-9; Sun. 12-5	VISA, MC, checks
Handicapped access: 1 step	
Other locations:	
8002 S.E. 13th	235-3287
Lake Oswego Village S/C	635-5326

CLASSIC PICTURE FRAMING

14672 S.E. McLoughlin Blvd.	653-2985
Hours: M, T, Th 10-7; W, F 10-9;	VISA, MC, checks
Sat. 10-5; Sun. 12-5	
Handicapped access: yes	
Other location:	
330 N. State Street, Lake Oswego	636-6518

FRAME FACTORY

211 N.W. Davis	228-1340
Hours: M-Sat. 10-5:30	VISA, MC, checks
Handicapped access: yes	

THE FRAME UP

1914 N.E. 122nd	253-2035
Hours: M-F 9:30-7, Sat. 10-5	VISA, MC, checks
Handicapped access: yes	

UP AGAINST THE WALL

219 N.W. Couch	223-9502
Hours: M-Sat. 11-7, F 11-9, Sun. 12-6	VISA, MC, checks
Handicapped access: yes	

Auctions

CITY OF PORTLAND PROPERTY AUCTIONS

1131 S.E. Powell   **248-4395**
Hours: Saturday   **Checks**
Handicapped access: yes

City of Portland auctions are held separately for surplus city property, stolen and unclaimed police property, and used city vehicles. City surplus property sales are held once a year to sell unwanted property ranging from desks and typewriters to old lawnmowers. Police property auctions occur 2 to 3 times a year, depending on how fast stolen and unclaimed property accumulates. Examples from a recent auction were: a chain saw ($150), a canoe with a bathtub thrown in "for the wife" ($167), a harp, 10 "no good" television sets ($2!), and a new, still-in-the-crate Magnavox television set ($220). Vehicles that have used up their easily-maintained life for the city are sold 4 or 5 times a year. Police sedans are sold after 70,000 miles, staff sedans after 80,000-100,000. No warranties are given or implied on any of the property, and the auctions are advertised on the radio and in local newspapers.

CLACKAMAS COUNTY PROPERTY AUCTION

902 Abernethy Rd., Oregon City   **655-8521**
Hours: Saturday   **Checks**
Handicapped access: yes

Clackamas County gets rid of its surplus equipment, vehicles, and office furniture once a year in the spring. The date is set according to the weather, since the auction is held outside near the Public Works Department shops. The auction is widely advertised in newspapers and on the radio.

MULTNOMAH COUNTY PROPERTY AUCTION

Exposition Center, 2060 N. Marine Dr.   **248-3350**
Hours: Saturday   **Checks**
Handicapped access: yes

Multnomah County holds public auctions about twice a year to sell surplus county property, unclaimed and stolen property amassed by the sheriff's department, and used county cars. The auctions take place on Saturdays, scheduled according to the quantity of items available for auction. A preview is held the day prior, and advertisements are placed in all major newspapers, on the radio, and sometimes on television. Previous buyers and those requesting it are sent auction announcements from a mailing list maintained by the county Office of Property Management. Items sold in the past have included stereo equipment, clothing, coins, radios, cookware, television sets, bayonets, and a case of Scotch whiskey. Best buys are on bicycles, cameras, and used county office furniture. Staff cars are sold at 70,000 miles and between 3 and 12 years of age. Patrol cars are also retired at 70,000 miles, but usually after only 2 years. One patrol car sold for $900, and a staff sedan, 5 years old, for $500 in August, 1979.

WASHINGTON COUNTY PROPERTY AUCTION

28th and N.E. Cornell Rd., Hillsboro   **648-8675**
Hours: Saturday   **Checks**
Handicapped access: yes

All county surplus items, vehicles, and confiscated goods from the sheriff's department are auctioned twice a year at the Washington County Fairgrounds in Hillsboro – usually the first Saturday in June and in December. Notices are run in all the local media.

Automotive Goods

(Also see Auctions)

BATTERY X-CHANGE

2930 S.E. 82nd	774-3131
Hours: M-F 8:30-5:30 Sat. 8:30-4	VISA, MC
Handicapped access: yes	
Other locations:	
12990 S.W. Canyon Road, Bvrt.	644-3425

Reconditioned batteries, alternators, starters, generators for cars, trucks, tractors, motorcycles, boats, golfcarts, snow-mobiles, aircraft, and trailers can be bought for about half the price of a new battery, and they all carry a one-year guarantee. As one salesman said, "They're fine, but I wouldn't buy one in the winter."

The best news is that they will buy used or broken batteries. Besides making you a little money, you're helping recycle some usable material and reducing the junk in the land fills. Prices, when we sold one, were $4.25 for a solid battery, and $3 for a broken one.

JOHN'S IMPORT AUTO WRECKING

733 N.W. Everett	222-1601
Hours: M-F 8-5:30, Sat. 8-3:30	VISA, MC, checks
Handicapped access: 6 steps	

When we had a spare tire stolen from the car, we bought a new tire and wheel for ¼ the price we would have had to pay for the same thing at a retail store. John's has 7 floors of imported wrecked autos, many with undamaged parts which he sells for less than half the new price. The sales people will find the part you wish and take it off the old body for you while you wait. The parts are guaranteed, but no cash refunds are given for returns. A 20% handling charge is added on all returned parts. The store also handles some new accessories and auto parts for imported cars.

OIL CAN HENRY'S

8350 S.E. Division	**771-1711**
Hours: M-Sat. 8-6	**VISA, MC, checks**
Other location:	
19026 S.E. Burnside	**666-9004**

Oil Can Henry's has applied the fast-food concept to oil changes and lube jobs. The service includes 5 quarts of Pennzoil, an oil filter, interior vacuuming, the windows washed, and a check and fill on all car fluids for $15.95. The best part is that it is all done in 10 minutes. That's about 2 hours and $5 better than at your local gas station. Owner Jeffry Dugan plans to open 15 shops in the Portland area.

RENT-A-JUNKER

3583 S.E. 82nd	**771-2273**
Hours: M-F 9-6, Sat. 10-4	**VISA, MC**

Need to get to the beach or the mountains, or just around town, and your car is in the shop? Rent-A-Junker is the answer. Nothing fancy, but for $7 a day, who's complaining? Cars range from 4 to 15 years old and rent for between $7 and $12 a day, with the first 50 miles included and 10 cents a mile after that. You must carry your own insurance and stay within a 100-mile radius of Portland with the cheaper cars. They all carry a 3-day minimum rental time.

STANDARD BATTERIES

3750 S.E. Belmont	**234-7251**
Hours: M-F 8-5	**VISA, MC, checks**
Handicapped access: yes	

Standard Batteries doesn't sell reconditioned batteries, but they will pay $3.25 for used ones, broken or unbroken.

UNITED BATTERY SYSTEMS

143 N.E. Columbia Blvd.	**289-6644**
Hours: M-Sat. 8-6	**VISA, MC**
Handicapped access: yes	
Other location:	
19001 E. Burnside	**667-9100**

Foreign and domestic batteries are bought and sold, as well

as generators, alternators, and starters. They are reconditioned there and resold with a year's guarantee. Some new batteries which are bought in volume are often available, and the price is somewhat less than retail because a year is dropped from the warranty.

Books

A AVATAR

5421 N.E. 33rd   287-3736
Hours: T-Sat. 10:30-6:30   Am. Exp., checks
Handicapped access: yes; stairs to 2nd floor

Mostly paperbacks are sold in this general interest used book store. Owner Ken Fritzler will trade similar books or magazines 2-for-1 and will sell books on consignment. He discounts prices for wholesalers or for quantity purchases. Paperbacks are all priced 40% below net cost.

ANGIE'S MAGAZINE RACK

2915 N.E. Broadway   288-4846
Hours: M-Sat. 12-6   Cash only
Handicapped access: 6 steps

Cramped quarters contain paperback books and magazines, including *National Geographic, Look,* and men's and women's selections. Owner Angelo Ardito will trade.

APACHE BOOKS AND BEDKNOBS

1509 S.E. Grand   235-4590
Hours: M-F 11-8, Sat. 10-6   Checks
Handicapped access: yes

Mostly paperback books – science fiction, Western, mystery, and general interest – are stocked in this warehouse-like store. Both old and new comic books (20,000 of them) are carried, and the owners will do some searches. They also buy, sell, and trade.

ARMCHAIR FAMILY BOOKSTORE

3205 S.E. Milwaukie   236-0270
Hours: M-F 10-9, Sat. 10-6   VISA, MC, checks
Handicapped access: yes

The 30,000-title inventory is divided between paperbacks,

comics, and magazines. An annual sale is held the week before Thanksgiving when credit slips good until January 1st are given to the customers: $5 credit to the first 10 people in the doors; $2 to everyone else.

BEAVER BOOK STORE

3747 S.E. Hawthorne   238-1668
Hours: M-Sat. 10-5:30   VISA, MC, checks
Handicapped access: yes

The store is stocked with half paperback, half hardback general, out-of-print, and old or rare books. Bargain tables are worth a look-through for books at 5/$1 and 7/$6. Owner Frank Isbell will trade.

BEAVERTON PAPERBACK

12620 S.W. 1st, Bvrt.   643-3537
Hours: M-F 10-5:30, Sat. 10-5   Checks
Handicapped access: yes

General interest selections are among the 100,000 paperbacks Jean McSweeny stocks. Buyers can trade 2-for-1.

BOOK BROWSE

922 N.W. 21st   223-4416
Hours: M-F 12-7, Sat. 12-6   VISA, checks
Handicapped access: yes

New and used books are among the 15,000-volume inventory of general interest books, many with a fine arts focus. Carol Nebel will do out-of-print searches and will special order books. She also carries cards, calendars, and bookmarks. Trading is possible.

BOOK HAVEN

8202 N. Denver   285-9493
Hours: M-Sat. 11-6   Checks
Handicapped access: yes

Paperbacks account for 75% of the 75,000 volumes of general interest stocked. Arthur Bucy will not trade but buys what he wants. He stamps his books with the store name, which may decrease the value of a rare edition, so the store is not for collectors. He also carries some magazines and has sections on the occult, metaphysics, and science fiction.

THE BOOK RACK

16441 S.E. Powell   **667-9669**
Hours: M-F 10-7, Sat. 10-6, Sun. 1-4   VISA, MC, checks
Handicapped access: yes

Juliette de Shetler will trade books or magazines 2-for-1. She carries about 25,000 volumes, mostly paperback, and about 4,000 comic books. A children's play area is provided for browsing parents. Half of the store is stocked with knitting machines and yarn for those with time to both read and knit.

BOOKS AND PRINTS

12680 S.W. Farmington, Bvrt.   **643-7222**
Hours: M-Sat. 10-6   **Checks**
Handicapped access: yes

Ernest and Margaret Ediger specialize in general interest hardcover books, with an 18,000-title inventory. They also carry some prints.

CAL'S BOOKS AND WARES

732 S.W. 1st   **222-5454**
Hours: M-F 10-5:30, Sat. 11-4   VISA, MC, checks
Handicapped access: stairs to 2nd floor

Calvin Hancock owns this antique-collectibles-bookstore and loves to talk to customers. The used books – 5,000 hardcover volumes – are upstairs and are mostly non-fiction, good quality books of general interest. He also carries some magazines. Besides the books, Cal stocks a small selection of vintage clothes and has some very good buys in furs. Some antique items are on consignment, and he won't dicker on those. However, he has been known to barter a bit on the items he owns.

CAMERON'S BOOKS AND MAGAZINES

336 S.W. 3rd   **228-2391**
Hours: M-Sat. 9-6   **Checks**
Handicapped access: yes

Advertised as Portland's oldest book store, Cameron's stocks an inventory of 20,000 paperback and hardback books at bargain prices. Bargain racks are on the sidewalk for lunch-time browsers. Owner Fred Goetz had Wayne Morse bumper stickers and pins, road maps, *National Geographic* magazines, maps, and a few records and comic books when we visited. He will search for a wanted volume.

CHRISTIAN DISCOUNT BOOK CENTER

4215 N.E. Hancock   **249-0267**
Hours: M-Th 9-6, F 9-8, Sat. 9-5   **VISA, MC, checks**
Handicapped access: yes

One of 11 outlets nationally with corporate headquarters in Grand Rapids, Michigan, the Christian Discount Book Center handles all new books at 10%-20% off list prices. Catalogs are available for mail ordering and contain discount coupons for some books.

CHRISTIAN SUPPLY CENTER

10209 S.E. Division   **256-4520**
Hours: M-F 9:30-9, Sat. 9:30-6   **VISA, MC, checks**
Handicapped access: yes

This large Christian book and supply store also stocks about 8,000 used, hardcover volumes. Owners are interested in buying or trading for all types of Christian books and often purchase the libraries of old estates. They will make an offer through the mail on individual books, as well as on sets and libraries, if title, author, publisher, edition, date, and condition are sent to them.

EXCALIBUR BOOKS

3849 S.E. Powell   **231-9809**
Hours: M-Sat. 10-6   **Checks**
Handicapped access: 2 steps inside

Kathleen Putnam stocks 50,000 copies of mostly paperback used science fiction, as well as some general interest volumes. Comics, *National Geographics,* and *Playboys* are also stocked. She will trade.

FUTURE DREAMS

1808 E. Burnside	231-8311
Hours: M-Sat. 12-6	VISA, MC, checks
Handicapped access: yes	

Science fiction, fantasy, and horror are the specialties here, plus an inventory of 10,000 comic books. Owners Don Riordon and Richard Finn also handle subscriptions for new comics and keep a box for each subscriber. When comic books arrive, they are put in each box, and the subscriber can pick them up at his leisure. Books will be traded usually 2-for-1. The store is clean and well-organized, and calendars, prints, posters, records, and cards (all with a fantasy theme) were stocked the day we visited.

GOLDEN AGE USED BOOKSTORE

4824 N. Lombard	283-9740
Hours: Every day 10-7	Checks
Handicapped access: yes	

Mostly fiction paperbacks are sold, none for more than $1. Science fiction is heavily stocked, as are comic books from as long ago as 1937. Owner Bruce Doering said he sold one collector comic book for $650. He will trade 2-for-1 of similar volumes. The store is closed some Sundays when he sells his books at the Coliseum Flea Market.

THE GREAT NORTHWEST BOOKSTORE

915 S.W. 9th	223-8098
Hours: M-Sat. 11-7	VISA, MC, checks
Handicapped access: steep ramp	

General interest books are stocked—some 40,000 copies of hardback and paperback, but owners Brian Trainer and Phil Wikelund are concentrating on literature, science fiction, and geography. They carry a few new books by local writers. They will trade, search, or special order.

GREEN DOLPHIN BOOKSTORE

215 S.W. Ankeny	224-3060
Hours: M-Sat. 11-9, Sun. 2-8	VISA, MC, checks
Handicapped access: step	

An inventory of 20,000 hardcover books is stocked, most falling into one of the advertised categories: "Northwest, West, modern first editions, books about books and book collecting, ships and the sea, curious and rare." Owner Wright Lewis also carries *National Geographic* magazines, a few maps, prints, pictures, pamphlets, and old letters. He will search for rare or out-of-print books, too.

KING OF ROME

8133 S.E. 13th   231-9270
Hours: M 1-6, T-Sun. 9:30-6   VISA, checks
Handicapped access: 1 step, narrow aisles

The store carries about 10,000 paperbacks, which can be traded 2-for-1, and about 2,000 hardcover titles, mostly nonfiction. Lots of records are stocked in all speeds, and owner Bill Mathews will trade on those, too. He also stocks all sorts of "collectibles," old prints, toys, and a few comic books.

OLD OREGON BOOK STORE

525 S.W. 12th   227-2742
Hours: M-Sat. 11-5   Checks
Handicapped access: yes

Phyllis and Preston McMann specialize in American history books. Their inventory of 100,000 titles covers Northwest subjects, scholarly books, some general interest, and some old and rare books.

THE OSWEGO POCKETBOOK EXCHANGE

148½ "B" Avenue, Lake Oswego   635-2872
Hours: M-Sat. 10:30-5:30   Checks
Handicapped access: yes

The Exchange has an inventory of 10,000 general interest paperbacks, a few records, and some comic books. The owner will buy, sell, and trade and is especially interested in buying older paperbacks.

THE PAPER MOON

3538 S.E. Hawthorne Blvd.   **236-5195**
Hours: M-Th 11:30-5; F-Sat. 12-5   **Checks**
Handicapped access: yes

Among the 10,000-title inventory are hardcover copies on literature, poetry, biography and photography (both photo albums and photographs). Andrea Drinard will do searches, and she carries children's books, old post cards, and some sheet music.

POWELL BOOKS

1005 W. Burnside   **228-4651**
Hours: M-Sat. 9-9, Sun. 12-6   **VISA, MC, checks**
Handicapped access: yes

The largest used bookstore in town has an amazing variety: 195,000 titles in every field, including a few new books. Walter W. Powell won't trade, but buys for cash and will add a bit more if you buy books for the amount of your sale to him. Dover books are a specialty.

SERENDIPITY CORNER

1401 S.E. Division   **233-9884**
Hours: M-Sat. 10-6   **VISA, MC, checks**
Handicapped access: yes

Science fiction and old and new comics are among the inventory of 100,000 books. Both hardback and paperback are stocked, mostly of general interest. Owner Jean Tader will trade 2-for-1 of the same value book.

Building Materials

BEE COMPANY — See Liquidators

BUILDER'S CITY

8905 N. Vancouver   **285-0546**
Hours: M-Sat. 9-5, Sun. 10-6   **VISA, MC, checks**
Handicapped access: 6 steps to main store, other areas OK

If you know what you need and are a good judge of quality in building materials, this 5-acre conglomeration of merchandise can be a good place to shop. Specializing in closeouts, bankruptcy stocks, overstocks, and damaged goods, Builders' City has a little bit of everything all the time, and a lot of some things sometimes. Doors, siding, lumber, paneling, hardware, insulation, plumbing and electrical supplies, and paint can all be found here. Some of the items are first quality; others (like the pile of plywood we saw which had been sitting in the rain for some time) may be cheap, but probably aren't worth much for more than the chicken coop. But then, the chickens won't care.

DEPOT FOR REUSEABLE BUILDING MATERIALS

721 S.E. Grand   **231-7430**
Hours: M-F 8:30-5   **Checks**
Handicapped access: upstairs, no elevator

Sponsored by the Human Resources Council of Oregon, the Depot is designed to recycle excess building materials and serve low-income homeowners and nonprofit agencies. All items are donated as a tax write-off and priced according to value and the ability of the buyer to pay.

Lumber, windows, paint, carpeting, cabinets, fluorescent light fixtures, and sliding glass doors have all moved through the warehouse. Some are new, some overstocks, others damaged or used. The value of the goods is considered to be half of the new, retail price. Low-income homeowners (those making a gross annual 1979 income of $7,975 or less) pay 25% of the value. Middle-income home-owners (those making up to

$13,000 annually) pay 75% of the value. Nonprofit groups with a building budget allowance under $500 pay 25%, with a budget over $500, 75%.

Interested persons should call the office during the week. The warehouse is open in Southeast Portland for pickups on Tues. and Thurs. from 8:30-5 and on Sat. from 9-4.

THE EXCHANGE

1616 N.W. 23rd   **221-0357**
Hours: M-F 8:30-5

The Exchange has taken the guilt out of having to get rid of usable, surplus junk. Acting as a clearinghouse for potential waste-swappers, the 3-year-old operation publishes a bulletin every 2 months listing waste products (mostly industrial types) such as wooden pallets, scrap metal, building materials, cardboard boxes, stained glass pieces, chemicals, and sludges.

The operation was started with a grant from the state Department of Environmental Quality, but when the grant expired, the Western Environmental Trade Association took over publication of the bulletin. You should call the Association to be placed on a mailing list for the bulletin or if you want to list something you have or need. Names are not published in the bulletin, and the Association makes all contacts between exchangers. Nothing is stored by the Association, since it now serves only as the clearinghouse for the potential exchanges, and no double checking or guarantees are made by the Association.

Even though we haven't needed anyone's surplus sludge yet, this sounds like a very useful, innovative way to save money and resources.

FACTORY CITY

110 S.E. Taylor   **238-2904**
Hours: M-Th 8-5:30, F 8-7, Sat. 8-5   **VISA, MC**
Handicapped access: 4 steps
Other location:
2815 S.E. 82nd   **777-5891**

Factory City carries a wide selection of building materials and appliances and usually has vast savings on items on which their buyers got a good deal or on damaged merchandise. Their prices on building materials and appliances are generally lower than elsewhere, but you can find some real buys in the Bargain Annex in the back of the building. No returns are allowed on the factory seconds, closeouts or damaged goods found there, but everything is out for easy inspection. When we visited, a factory-direct, first quality shipment of 2,000 sliding aluminum windows was selling for 65% off the manufacturer's suggested list price and 30% less than Factory City's normal price. Odds and ends, like mouldings—20 pieces for $1, door jambs—30¢ a linear foot, and odd-sized doors were especially good buys in the Annex.

IMPERIAL PAINTS FACTORY STORE

11716 S.E. Division   **760-2912**
Hours: M-F 7:30-5:30, Sat. 9-1   **VISA, MC, checks**
Handicapped access: yes
Other location:
2526 N.W. Yeon   **228-0207**

Faced with a motto like "Our paint store is solvent," how can the buyer go wrong? The outlet store serves contractors as well as the general public, and the larger discounts are offered on volume purchases. Closeout sales offer discounts of up to 50% on a gallon. Gallons of discontinued colors and color "mistakes" are also sold for half off, but the "mistakes" are usually only available a gallon at a time. Bulk thinner (you bring the container) sells for $1 a gallon. Any paint purchased in 5-gallon buckets is 15 cents a gallon cheaper, with greater discounts for purchases of 25 gallons or more. All paint supplies are carried, including competitive brands (at no discount), and wallpaper is 20% off the book prices.

CABINET WAREHOUSE

1305 S.E. Union   **238-3963**
Hours: F-M 9-5   **VISA, MC, checks**
Handicapped access: yes

Cash and carry is the byword of this former distributor of appliances and cabinetry which recently opened to the public after its Anchorage outlet began getting merchandise direct from the factory. Admiral and O'Keefe-Merritt appliances will not be restocked after the present merchandise is sold, but the warehouse-full should remain for more than a year at savings of 25%-60% off list price. Excel brand kitchen and bathroom cabinets will remain the main feature of Cabinet Warehouse, with savings of up to 60%.

MR. PLYWOOD

9275 S.W. Canyon Rd.	**297-1851**
Hours: M-F 8-9, Sat. 8-5:30,	**VISA, MC, checks**
Sun. 9-5:30	
Handicapped access: yes	
Other locations:	
7609 S.E. Stark	**254-7387**
16420 S.E. McLoughlin Blvd., Milw.	**653-5401**

The best buy here is paneling: Mr. Plywood has the largest selection and supply, and because of the volume, the best prices in town. Full units of plywood and paneling are discounted an additional 5% from the piece price. The store is geared to the do-it-yourselfer, and home tinkerers can have a heyday sorting through the "shop grades" (corners nicked, edges rough) for a 25% discount, and the even cheaper "blows" (lamination coming apart). Although the latter are not often as useful as the shop grade merchandise, if you have a small job that requires less than a full 8' x 4' sheet of plywood or paneling, it can be done for a little less.

Check the "u-pick" bin for closeout, discontinued, or last-of-a-unit merchandise for up to a 50% discount. The Formica sink cutouts are very cheap and can be cut to make small bathroom countertops for less than $1. Service is quick, friendly, and knowledgeable, and a liberal cash refund policy is maintained. The open display and self-selection make browsing a possibility not found at most lumberyards. However, lumber is about the only thing they aren't competitive on, so check the lumberyards for that.

STANDARD BRANDS PAINT CO.

20 N.E. Hancock	**287-8098**
Hours: M-F 8-9, Sat. 8-6:30,	**VISA, MC, checks**
Sun. 9-5:30	
Handicapped access: yes	
Other location:	
11424 S.E. 82nd, Milw.	**653-5311**

We love these places where we can bring our own container

to be refilled at a savings not only to us but of the world's nonrenewable resources. Standard Brands is another place to get a refill of paint thinner. Besides that, everything in the store is marked down from 10%-50% below regular retail price because of volume buying for the 78 nationwide stores. The store manager said he watches advertisements in the papers and will match any other store in town. Paints, ladders, tile, carpeting, wallpaper, art supplies, crafts, picture frames, and glass cut to size free of charge are all available. Plenty of uniformed salespeople are knowledgeable and ready to help. But they leave you alone until you ask for help by taking a number at the central sales desk.

Grumbacher art supplies, among other brands, were 20% less than we found in specialty art supply stores.

Catalog Discounters

Mail-order houses of name-brand merchandise have showrooms where savings can be found on items ranging from Samsonite luggage to Wilson tennis balls. Small appliances, jewelry, photography and stereo equipment, sporting goods, and china are sold at about 20% below list price (and usually at least a few dollars less than in department stores). Catalogs are available by mail, and either mail orders or phone orders will be taken. The showrooms are spacious and modern, much like department stores, except that you don't take the display item off the shelf. You fill out an order form and wait for a boxed item to be brought from the adjoining warehouse. At Christmastime this can take up to an hour, but a phone order or stopping back later to pick up the item can save some waiting time.

DAHNKEN, INC.

1620 N.E. 122nd   **255-2274**
Hours: M-Th 10-6, F 10-9, Sat. 10-5   **VISA, MC, checks**
Handicapped access: yes

Located in the San Rafael Shopping Center. No cash refunds are made, but exchanges may be made within 10 days of purchase if the original box and the receipt are saved.

JAFCO, INC.

10500 S.W. Beaverton-Hillsdale Hwy., Bvrt.   **643-6771**
Hours: M-F 10-9, Sat. 9-6, Sun. 11-6   **VISA, MC, checks**
Handicapped access: yes
Other locations:
16250 S.E. McLoughlin Blvd., Milw.   **653-2500**
2095 E. Burnside, Gresham   **667-5500**
619 S.W. Alder   **221-0844**

A chain of 12 stores in Oregon and Washington, Jafco continually has attractive prices and good sales. Aggressive merchandising as well as convenience have added to its already attractive prices. We buy our Kodak film and mailers here, having found them 20% less than most other places. Cash refunds are made; however approval must be received before returning mail orders. Gift certificates are available, too. The downtown store carries exclusively stereos and photo equipment. The other stores are catalog showrooms where a wide variety of items are displayed.

Clothing

(Also see Liquidators, Sporting Goods,
Thrift Shops, Flea Markets, Rummage Sales)

Men's and Women's New

CINDERELLA SAMPLES

8101 S.E. Stark   252-0408
Hours: M-F 9:30-5:30, Sat. 9:30-5   VISA, MC, checks
     (opens at 10 during daylight saving time)
Handicapped access: yes

Most of the name-brand women's wear salesmen's samples
sold here are 15% off regular retail prices, and sizes range
from 7-18. The shopper should be aware, however, that several
brands (LeMar, Candi Jones, and Gunnysax) are not sample
merchandise and sell at regular retail prices. These are mixed
on the racks with samples, so bargain buying can be confusing,
and price comparison is a must. All sales are final, but layaway
is available.

C.Y.'s HOUSE OF SAMPLES

6800 N.E. Killingsworth   287-5770
Hours: T-F 12-9, Sat. 10-5:30   VISA, MC, checks
Handicapped access: yes

This store features the biggest selection of name-brand sample clothes in the Portland area. Men's, women's, and children's
and infant's clothes, from formal wear to jogging outfits, are all
reasonably marked. When we were there, Head, Pacific Trail,
and White Stag skiwear was marked 40% off suggested retail;
other names were 60% off retail. Munsingwear socks were
marked down 30%; ties were half price. Sizes tend toward the
average (9-10 for women), but generally a wide selection is
available.
     The store is very crowded, both with merchandise and peo-
ple, and bargains are definitely worth any hassle. Several fit-

ting rooms are available, and returns and layaways are permitted.

DANNER SHOE MFG. CO

Omark Industrial Park, off Oregon 224   **653-2920**
Hours: M-Sat. 9-5, F 9-9   **VISA, MC, checks**
Handicapped access: curb

The retail store for Danner hiking and work boots has few seconds ("We try not to") but they usually have one or two pairs in the store, so it's worth checking. The boots are worth buying anyway for the quality, but you might as well save 20% when you can. Customer returns are also marked 20% off, and an annual clearance sale near Thanksgiving puts most of the stock at the same reduction. You won't get the savings, and you will have to pay an additional $10, but the factory will make special sizes if you don't have feet that fit society's norm. Mail order catalog is available, and if the factory is out of the ordered size or style, it will make it up within 6 weeks.

DOANE'S SHOE BOX

7116 N.E. Sandy   **282-6845**
Hours: M-Sat. 9:30-6   **VISA, MC, checks**
Handicapped access: yes

This 12-year-old merchandiser of shoes from bankrupt stores offers great savings on a number of brands. We found Naturalizer, Airstep, Willco, DeLiso, Joyce and Caress when we visited, in sizes from 5-10. They try to keep prices from $7-$10 below what the shoe would sell for in normal retail outlets. A January sale brings all shoe prices to between $10-$20. A large selection of fancy gold and silver shoes and handbags was also stocked.

J. GARRISON'S

4949 S.W. 76th   **292-2747**
Hours: M-Sat. 10-6, Sun. 12-5   **VISA, MC, checks**
Handicapped access: curb

Joyce Hoffman stresses personalized service in her high fashion discount women's clothing store in Raleigh Hills. The same designer labels found in downtown boutiques – Halston, Von Furstenberg, Klein, Lauren, Vanderbilt – are here for at least 25% less and sometimes as much as half price. She says she has lower overhead, buys for less from the manufacturer, and accepts no returns, so she can keep her prices down. She keeps a mailing list and will call frequent customers when something in their size comes in. A television set and a play area accommodate the accompanying husband and kids. Definitely a place to check before any expensive suit, dress, or formal is bought. January sales lower prices even more.

KANDEL KNITTING MILLS FACTORY OUTLET

4834 N. Interstate   **288-6975**
Hours: M-F 9-4   **VISA, MC, checks**
Handicapped access: yes

This small factory specializes in school athletic sweaters, shirts, and jackets, but does make some other styles which they sell at wholesale prices in the factory outlet. The 100% wool sweaters are very reasonably priced. A huge box in one corner holds cut-out sweater pieces that were never sewn together – bodies and arms – for $2/lb.

MEIKO'S

8765 S.W. Canyon Lane   **297-2004**
Hours: T-Sat. 11-6, Th 11-7   **VISA, MC, checks**
Handicapped access: yes

Name-brand and designer fashions from overstock, surplus, and closeout lines are sold here at savings from 10%-60% off the list price. Louella Eisenbraun scrounges for whatever high fashion women's clothes she can find at a good price, and everything is new and in first quality condition. She will hold clothes on layaway and make exchanges, but no cash refunds are permitted. Sizes range from pre-teen to size 20, though most women's clothes are sizes 9-12.

Louella also sells handmade Thai silk dresses and blouses which she designs. Her sister, who lives in Thailand, has the dresses and blouses made up there. Though not inexpensive, Louella says they are much less than elsewhere because she has eliminated the middlemen. She notifies regular customers of special sales and new shipments via her mailing list, so be sure to sign the register when you shop.

NORDSTROM'S CLOTHES RACK

1014 Lloyd Center   **287-2444**
Hours: M-F 9:30-9,   **VISA, MC, Nordstrom's, checks**
        Sat. 9:30-6, Sun. 12-5
Handicapped access: yes

Items that have been reduced to clear and special purchases
are sold in a crowded little room on the lower level of the Lloyd
Center Nordstrom's store. Men's and women's and some
children's clothing are sold there, often at less than ½ the
former price.

PENDLETON WOOLEN MILLS
FACTORY OUTLET

217th, Washougal, Washington   **226-4801 (in Portland)**
Hours: M-F 8-4   **Checks**
Handicapped access: yes

Though this factory outlet is outside the area covered in the
rest of the book, it is close enough and too good not to include.
Take I-5 north from Portland to the Camas exit, continue to
Washougal, and watch for the Pendleton Woolen Mills water
tower. The sales room is in the parking lot. Clothing, fabric,
blankets, thread, and even the old wooden thread spools are for
sale. All items are seconds or irregulars, but many of the flaws
are invisible. If you are headed east on 80-N, stop by and check
out the factory outlet store in Pendleton, Oregon. It stocks
mainly blankets but has some clothes. A call to either store
ahead of time is wise if you are looking for something specific.

PIC-A-DILLY

1830 N.E. 122nd   **256-9171**
Hours: M-F 10-9, Sat. 9:30-6, Sun. 12-5   VISA, MC, checks
Handicapped access: yes, turnstile inside
Other locations:
15830 S.E. McLoughlin Blvd.   **653-9224**
1615 N.E. 21st   **288-1318**
Also in Lloyd Center, Vancouver, Gresham, & Beaverton

This western chain of discount women's clothing now counts
175 stores in 8 states and is adding 50 new stores a year. Well
organized with savings advertised from 30%-50%, the store
buys first quality name-brand junior fashions from overstocked

manufacturers, buys in bulk, and has low overhead in all stores, thereby keeping the prices down. Sizes are generally 3-16, though a few things will go to size 20. Selection is vast though limited to good contemporary looks – nothing high fashion. Check the under-$2 table for accessories such as sunglasses, purses, and scarves. Two clearance sales a year cut all prices by ⅓. Sales are well advertised in local papers. No refunds, but exchanges or credit will be made on purchases returned within 7 days.

SALLY'S CLOTHES OUT

2548 S.E. 122nd	**760-2277**
Hours: M-F 10-8, Sat. 10-6, Sun. 11-4	**VISA, MC, checks**
Handicapped access: yes	
Other locations:	
7776 S.W. Capitol Hwy.	**244-6403**
7000 S.E. Thiessen Rd., Milw. (Westwood S/C)	**653-5522**

There's no Sally here – the owner's name is Pat – she just thought Sally sounded good. Savings of 40%-70% are advertised on women's and junior wear that is new from overstocks and a few salesmen's samples. Sizes run from 3-20 on brands such as Jantzen, Ship 'n Shore, Bobby Brooks, Catalina. A rack of leather coats had some good selections for under $50. Exchanges are OK, and dressing rooms are available.

THE SAMPLE NOOK

6315 S.W. Capitol Hwy.	**246-9363**
Hours: M-Sat. 9:30-5:30	**VISA, MC, checks**
Handicapped access: curb	

Dorothy Wollner has run her little Hillsdale hole-in-the-wall for 11 years selling salesmen's samples. She says she starts prices at ⅓ less than what retail stores will price for the same clothes, and some are marked down as much as 50%. Styles and sizes range from misses to "large and older," and quality is middle of the road – a lot of polyester. Because they are samples, most items are one-of-a-kind, and often of one size, but a size 7 should have luck almost anytime. Fitting rooms are available, but returns are not.

SAMPLES ONLY

20 N.W. 2nd	222-1784
Hours: T-Sat. 10-6	VISA, MC, checks
Handicapped access: yes	

Men's, women's, and boy's clothing are sold here at wholesale or slightly above wholesale prices. The women's samples run from size 7-12, the men's appeared to be more concentrated around 40 for coats and 32-34 for pants. The clothes are in first-rate condition and in fashionable styles. Wrangler and Haggar brands were abundant when we visited. Dressing rooms are available. Exchanges will be made but no refunds.

THE SHOE FACTORY

1840 N.E. 122nd	255-1254
Hours: M-F 10-9, Sat. 10-6, Sun. 12-5	VISA, MC, checks
Handicapped access: curb	
Other locations:	
Cedar Hills S/C, Bvrt.	297-5041

Co-owner Ed LaFrance was in the "legitimate" shoe business for many years before he opened his brand-name clearinghouse 3 years ago. His business satisfies both the wise shopper and the manufacturers who get stuck with late shipments or excess inventories. Customers will find names like Amalfi, Naturalizer, Grasshopper, and Pappagallo selling for $10-$25 less a pair than their retailed counterparts. Semiannual clearance sales cut prices up to 80%, and a mailing list of preferred customers gives a 2-day early selection. LaFrance said he sells 4,000 pairs of shoes every month. All shoes are on racks for customer self-selection and fitting. A full line of men's and women's shoes are available, as well as hiking boots, but no children's shoes are carried.

THE YELLOW BALLOON

15450 S.W. Boones Ferry Rd.	636-7485
Hours: M-Sat. 10-6	VISA, MC, checks
Handicapped access: yes	

First-quality sportswear, from warm-ups and ski clothes to women's White Stag blazers and slacks, are discounted from one-third to one-half off the tagged prices. The original prices of the White Stag, Head, and Wrangler brands are left on so you can see the savings. The small store, which stocks mostly women's clothes (but does carry some men's ski clothes and warm-ups and some children's ski clothing), makes its money by buying overstocks and closeouts. Junior sizes run from 3-15, women's from 6-20 and the rest from small to X-large. They will give credit or exchanges, and sales bring prices even lower sometimes.

Retro

Why buy the "look" of the '40s when you can buy the real thing? Luckily, fashion runs in cycles and what was brand new 30 or 40 years ago, is back in style for the '80s.

The retro resale shops capitalize on this fact of fashion and owners forage in closets, attics, trunks, and warehouses to get not only the look, but the feel of the fine rayons, gabardine, and angora wools and pure cottons that were used in the pre-polyester days. Waists might have to be tucked or loosened, hems adjusted, but since the inherent quality of the garment is usually good, savings can be fantastic.

Most stores carry women's clothing, shoes, jewelry, and hats, and many have men's suits and accessories. Tuxedos can be found in unbelievable styles.

Oregon law requires that all used clothing be dry cleaned before going on the racks, so a buyer shouldn't feel squeamish about buying someone else's clothing.

THE BLUE GARDENIA

222 W. Burnside   **226-0136**
Hours: M-Sat. 11-5:30, Sun. 12-4   VISA, MC, checks
Handicapped access: yes

Since 1975 the young shoppers seeking the vintage look in clothes have been invading Skid Road on West Burnside to shop at one of Portland's first retro resale shops. The small shop carries a good line of women's and men's clothes, the latter mainly suits, sport jackets, and Hawaiian print shirts. Styles up to the 1950's are stocked, along with a few new items that match the retro look. The owner also runs Keep 'Em Flying in Northwest Portland, but tries to keep all the natural fibers and specialty items at the Blue Gardenia store. All sales are final, though she does allow layaway and has gift certificates.

CAL'S BOOKS AND WARES—See Used Books

THE FADED ROSE

211 S.W. 6th   223-6430
Hours: M-Sat. 11-5   Checks
Handicapped access: yes

Stylish vintage clothing dating from 1900 to the 1950's is in good supply mainly for women of medium sizes. Prices are commensurate with contemporary consignment shops, and some very interesting pieces are available. A black beaded '40s dress for $40, a long, knit fringed dress from the '20s for $25 were some of the bargains when we visited. Shoes, hats, gloves, men's shoes, hats, socks, and suits are all available. Clothes on consignment pay 30% to the store. Refunds will be made if merchandise is brought back the same day only, but layaway is available.

FANDANGO

834 S.W. 10th   No phone
Hours: M-F 11-2, 3-5; Sat. 12-4   Checks
Handicapped access: yes

We saw some good names in women's suits here: Bullocks, Lipman Wolfe, Charles Berg and some Meier and Frank pieces. The store stocks mostly 1940's clothes for women, though there were a few Hawaiian print shirts, robes, and suits for men when we visited. Several seamstresses sell handmade clothes in retro looks, often made from original fabric and patterns. The owner will hold merchandise for 24 hours and a layaway up to one month. All sales are final.

JOHNNIE B. GOODE'S ROCK 'N' ROLL FASHIONS

832 S.W. Park   227-7772
Hours: M-Sat. 11-5   Checks
Handicapped access: yes

This retro shop is specializing in what they call "avant garde"—lamé, leopard coats, and furs. But they also stock a number of practical suits, skirts, and blouses. The era is 1940-1959, and wool, rayon, and 100% cotton abound. Both men's and women's styles are stocked. Prices are not of the "thrift shop" range, but quality is better. Large sizes are abundant, but some 5's and 7's are available. All sales are final, and they will look for specialty items for a customer and call when they find it.

KEEP 'EM FLYING

510 N.W. 21st   221-0601
Hours: M-Sat. 9-6   VISA, MC, checks
Handicapped access: yes

The nostalgic look is on the retail racks in department stores, but a little browsing through resale stores like Keep 'em Flying will turn up less expensive originals out of rayon, angora rabbit, and even silk. Hats are a real find here, and while prices are not as low as other consignment shops, the clothes have a lot of style. The store also carries an interesting supply of old patterns for those who want to sew their own. Credit is given on returns.

ONE MORE TIME

1114 N.W. 21st Ave.   223-4167
Hours: M-F 11-5, Sat. 11-6   VISA, MC, checks
Handicapped access: yes

Randy Greenlee prefers to call her merchandise "quality previously-owned" rather than resale or used. She carries a generous supply of both men's and women's vintage looks and has expanded to give the men their own adjacent store. Though prices vary according to quality, Randy says she prices at least 1/3 less than similar quality in retail stores. Her interest is in making a complete look and she holds monthly seminars with United Hair Force, a hair and makeup studio, in which customers are given free lessons in makeup application and hair design to match the '40s and '50s look of the clothes they are buying. She also caters to those looking for costumes, to theater groups and antique car clubs.

Seamstresses will sew old patterns with new materials for custom orders and for the store racks. Exchanges, but no refunds on returns.

SARMA'S RETRO SHOPPE

2001 S.W. 6th   222-2573

Hours: T-F 10:30-6, Sat. 11-5   **VISA, MC, checks**
Handicapped access: 6 steps

Sarma was a Portland State University business major when she brought the rhinestone look to the university area. The store is not a consignment shop; Sarma scrounges at estate sales, auctions, and in attics for her merchandise. She cleans, mends, presses, and accessorizes the clothes before they hit the racks, and renovates some garments completely – turning a stained skirt into the perfect vest. She will also make up clothes from old patterns for her customers. Wool sweaters and skirts were $7-$10; a black lace '40's evening gown was priced at $48 when we visited. Some of the shoes from the 1920's were still in their original boxes, and 1940's dresses had the tags hanging in the sleeves. she generally discourages returns and exchanges, but will allow layaways with a percentage of the price to hold an item.

THE SEWING CIRCLE

1034 S.W. 3rd   **227-7985**
Hours: M-Sat. 11-6   **Checks**
Handicapped access: one step
The Sewing Circle Annex, 1012 S.W. 3rd   **223-1977**

Both men's and women's clothing can be found at this vintage-wear store which has expanded to the annex 2 doors down 3rd Avenue. Some new items that fit the vintage look, besides older and some handmade items, are a little higher priced than other resale shops, but they are still less than retail – at least 50% less. Selection of men's suits was good and well priced, averaging about $15. Women's jeans were $6-$8, and an angora rabbit sweater in very good condition was $20. The store has two 25%-off sales in August and February to clear seasonal stock. A 35% commission is charged on all consigned clothing as well as on those that are custom made. If you have a pattern, material, and notions, the store's tailors can make an outfit for $3.75 an hour plus the store's commission. Exchanges are allowed if merchandise is returned within one day. Fitting rooms and layaway also are available.

THE SHADY LADY

823 N.W. 23rd   **248-0518**

Hours: M-Sat. 11-6:30   VISA, MC, checks
Handicapped access: yes

This non-consignment resale store was strictly vintage-look
when we visited, offering some elegant and interesting pieces
from the 1900s. But Princess Batway, the owner, said she
planned to change it to punk. She had already adopted the mul-
ti-hued red, green, pink, and blue hair and was beginning to call
herself Batwoman. An entire warehouse stock of Levi's from
the last time "cigaret jeans" were in style still had the original
labels and were at Levi's, not Calvin Klein's, prices. She also
stocks items she thinks match what she calls a "classic"
look – women's silk pleated tuxedo shirts with black ties she
was selling for about ½ price. Costuming people for parties is
her favorite pastime, and she says she can make a complete
look for under $35. She also will rent clothes to those she can
trust, but refunds on sales are not made.

218 CLOTHIERS

218 S.W. Broadway   241-3085
Hours: M-Sat. 11-6   VISA, checks
Handicapped access: yes

With the coming of the 1980's, "retro" now includes the '50's,
and this shop has just recently jumped on the retro bandwagon.
Concentrating on the New Wave look – go go boots, leather
jackets, Suzie Wong mini-skirts, plastic mini-dresses with zippers – the two owners also carry almost anything they find and
like. That includes big, bulky-knit sweaters that have also hit
the department stores and very fashionable suits. We found a
Davidow 3-piece wool suit priced at $26. They are not afraid to
dicker on the prices, and are eager to please the customer. Different items are put on sale all the time; men's shirts were
marked down 20% when we were there. No cash refunds are
made.

Consignment Resale

ACT II

1139 S.W. Morrison   227-7969
Hours: T-Sat. 10-4:30   VISA, MC, checks
Handicapped access: yes

"Next to new but new to you" is Ella Director's motto for her fashionable resale shop, and her merchandise upholds her goal of offering high quality women's clothing for low prices. Names like Anne Klein, Diane Von Furstenberg, Liz Claiborn, Miss Magnin, and Albert Nipon peek from rack after rack with prices set at least half off the original price, much lower than today's prices. She puts clothes on the racks as consignors bring them in, so you might find a summer dress for that Christmas Hawaiian trip. Prices are set by her according to quality with no set percentage off, but she does lower prices as merchandise sits. Most sales are final, but she will make exchanges or give credit at times, and layaway is available. The atmosphere is much like a small clothing salon, with adequate mirrors, dressing rooms, and the merchandise conveniently priced, sized, and arranged. Sizes range from 4-20.

CARRIE B'S

5701 N.E. Fremont   **284-0061**
Hours: T-Sat. 10-5:30   **VISA, MC, checks**
Handicapped access: two steps

Mary Kay Jones says she is sure hers is the only resale shop for square-dance clothes in the Northwest. The back of her small 4-year-old shop is full of the full-skirted ginghams and petticoats that swirl and sashay – most of them made by square dancers. The frilly petticoats, which can run to $50 retail, can be found for about 75% off. The front of the store features resale women's clothing, sizes 6-18, with the bulk in the mid-sizes. We found a Diane Von Furstenberg label and a never-worn 3-piece outfit from Tahiti – halter, short skirt, and long skirt – for $35. The tags on it were marked $88. All sales are final.

THE CLOTHES CLOSET

425 S.W. 2nd, Lake Oswego   **636-5932**
Hours: T-Sat. 10-5:30   **VISA, MC, checks**
Handicapped access: curb

Located in the Country Square Shopping Center, the store has thrived for almost 20 years on society women who follow the fashions and recycle their clothes. Former Lake Oswego residents send their clothes from Hawaii, the coast, and Seattle for 50% of the selling price. Oscar de la Renta, Gunnysax, Von Furstenberg, and Lanz can be found from 10%-25% of retail, though the more expensive pieces can be as high as 50% of the original price. A few unworn pieces, still with the tags, can be found, too.

Seasonal clothes stay on the racks throughout the season, which can be a boon to those who like to buy summer clothes in August. An eye to the local newspaper ads is wise, as the store does not have a mailing list. All sales are final, but layaway is available. Sizes range from 3-22.

ELEGANT EWE

828 S.W. 10th   **227-7278**
Hours: M-F 10-4   **VISA, MC, checks**
Handicapped access: 1 step

This well-organized consignment resale store carries only women's clothes. Prices are usually set at ⅓ of the original price. Sizes run from 6-22. Lee Mar, Koret of California, Lanz Originals, Act II, and Alex Coleman dresses were on the racks when we visited. All sales are final.

JULIE'S RESALE

6920 N.E. Sandy Blvd.   **284-1336**
Hours: M, W-Sat. 10:30-5   **VISA, MC, checks**
Handicapped access: yes

Designer labels such as Lordleigh, Jantzen, and Von Furstenberg are available for vastly reduced prices the second time around. Prom dresses are in abundance, as well as scarves and shoes in this women's store. Sizes range from 3-20 with emphasis on the mature woman in size and style. All sales are final.

THE LITTLE ROOM

811 N. Killingsworth   **289-8044**
Hours: M-Sat. 9-5   **Checks**
Handicapped access: yes

This small, resale consignment store carries women's, men's, and some children's clothing in limited variety and quality.

Prices were good, commensurate with thrift shops. Check it out for those annually-needed prom dresses. A fitting room is available, but all sales are final.

THE LITTLE RUMMAGE SHOP

1410 N.E. Broadway   **287-7821**
Hours: W-Sat. 12-5   **Checks**
Handicapped access: yes

The sign outside says, "Let me sell your old fur coats," which is what the owners have been doing for the last 4 years in this tiny storefront stuffed with resale and sample clothing, a few dishes, and some furniture. Everything is on consignment at 50-50 terms. Its location on a major arterial and near other shopping makes it easy to stop by to check bargains on your way to or from.

RAGS TO RICHES

4916 S.E. Division   **236-8465**
Hours: M-F 10:30-5:30, Sat.,   **VISA, MC, checks**
**   Sun. 10:30-5**
Handicapped access: yes
Other location:
11239 S.E. Division   **253-3779**

Prices on the men's and women's consignment clothing are split 50-50 with the store. Clothes are mostly mid-quality, though a few name brands were noticed. Sizes range up to 20. Best buys are bridal gowns and veils—all new, overstocks, or discontinued models—selling for 50% of retail. All sales are final, but layaway is available.

THE RESALE RACK

12190 S.E. Market   **253-9206**
Hours: M-F 9:30-6, Sat. 9:30-5   **VISA, MC, checks**
Handicapped access: yes

Men's, women's, and children's clothing are sold on consignment. Sizes for women range from juniors to queensize. Clothes are generally of medium quality—a good place to buy that polyester pantsuit at a low price. Jeans were about $5, men's suits around $30. All sales are final.

RITA'S RACK

3583 N.E. Broadway   287-0646
Hours: T-Sat. 10:30-5   Checks
Handicapped access: up stairs

Rita Coss and her mother, Mary Jane Groce, have turned an old house into a consignment store for women's clothing. Rita said she will only accept clothing in style that is clean and on hangers, and she keeps up her end of the bargain by neatly arranging and pricing clothes. Her prices seemed quite low, and she said she is trying to stay below other resale stores. The Bargain Room upstairs offers more savings on lower quality goods. Sizes from 5-22, layaway available, all sales final.

SALLY'S RESALE BOUTIQUE

3735 S.E. Hawthorne Blvd.   238-6732
Hours: M-Sat. 10:30-5:30   VISA, MC, checks
Handicapped access: yes

Men's, women's, and children's clothing are all available at this large consignment clothing shop. Prom dresses, accessories, and even corsets are marked about 10% of retail. Everything was sized—something not found in all resale shops. Consignment is split 50-50, and all sales are final. Items are accepted only on a seasonal basis, so clearance sales are held every 3 months. Watch for ads in local newspapers.

WHY NOT SHOP

8000 N.E. Glisan   253-5554
Hours: T-Sat. 10-5   VISA, MC, checks
Handicapped access: yes

This small women's resale shop stresses middle-of-the-road clothes with average prices. We found a very nice pair of fine wool pants for $10, and a 3-piece corduroy suit for $11. All sales are final, and layaway is available.

Y'S BUYS

1127 S.W. Morrison   222-2669
Hours: M-F 10-3:45   Cash only
Handicapped access: yes

The YWCA accepts both consignment and donated clothing and other small items to raise money for their summer camp, Westwind. Rules on consignment are strict as far as cleanliness, and everything is nicely organized and conveniently priced. A new woman's polyester suit was marked 50% from the original price tag. Check the sale rack for things that have been in the store more than 30 days. All sales are final, and layaway is not available.

Children's

JAYVEE BRAND, INC. — See Fabrics

KID STUFF

240 Tigard Plaza, S.W. Pacific Hwy.	**620-1273**
Hours: M-Th, Sat. 9:30-6, F 9:30-9	**VISA, MC, checks**
Handicapped access: yes	

This delightful store is bursting with bargains on quality new infant's and children's clothing, almost all at least 15% below retail prices and many regularly ⅓ off. Buying in volume and from salesmen keeps the prices down. Sizes run from toddler to children's 14-16, and common brands are Cinderella, Pacific Trail, Kate Greenaway, Health-tex, Carter. Bonnie Doon socks were 15% off when we were there. Layaway is available and 2 fitting rooms provided.

WEE THREE

4825 S.W. Hall, Bvrt.	**644-5953**
Hours: M-F 9-5, Sat. 10-5	**VISA, MC, checks**
Handicapped access: 4 steps	

Kids grow out of their clothes so fast they sometimes don't wear them out. Wee Three offers a place to sell your children's out-grown clothes and to buy the next size larger. Sales are split 50-50 on clothing; toys and baby equipment such as baby cribs draw 60% for the consignor; handcrafts and gifts bring 70%. Carefully selected, these are top quality items selling for ½ of the new retail price. Sizes are infant to 12, and layaway is possible.

Fabrics

(Also see Liquidators, Sporting Goods)

AMERICAN FABRICS

308 N.W. 11th   **222-3665**
Hours: M-F 9:30-5:30, Sat. 10:30-3:30   **VISA, MC, checks**
Handicapped access: yes

Low overhead and volume purchasing allow this long-established vendor of upholstery and auto fabric, drapery material, and wallpaper to offer discounts of 10%-20% off normal retail. A large selection is stacked and hung in every available inch of the store making browsing difficult, but sample books may be checked out for more leisurely looking. Upholstery brands such as Elko, Waverly, J.P. Marian, and Milehigh are 20% off retail, including special orders. Kirsch drapery hardware sells for 10% off retail. Orders can be filled within a week to 10 days. Returns are allowed on flawed merchandise.

BITS AND PIECES — See Interior Decorating

CALICO CORNERS

8526 S.W. Terwilliger Blvd.   **244-6700**
Hours: M-Sat. 9:30-5:30   **VISA, MC, checks**
Handicapped access: curb

This outlet for drapery and upholstery fabric advertises its wares as "carefully selected seconds . . . from the bluebloods of the industry," and satisfied customers confirm that boast. Display racks from floor to ceiling exhibit yardage arranged neatly by color for easy view and choice. Materials range from vinyls to sheers to hand-embroidered crewels from India. All are about 50% below retail. Bolt ends of up to 10 yards are marked down another $1-$2.

The store also sells some trims at 5% off normal retail and stocks some drapery and upholstery notions at retail price. Feather throw pillows (uncovered) ranged from $7.75 to $18.75 for sizes from 12-20 inches the day we visited.

A special August sale is held each year with savings of up to 60%, and a mailing list is kept to notify customers of sales and shipments. All sales are final, with no returns of either cut or uncut goods.

DISCOUNT FABRICS

210 Tigard Plaza, S.W. Pacific Hwy.   639-2434
Hours: M-F 9:30-9, Sat. 9:30-6, Sun. 12-5   VISA, MC, checks
Handicapped access: yes
Other locations:
11 others in Portland area—check Yellow Pages—Fabrics

This full-line fabric store offers an array of clothing, camping, upholstery, and drapery fabrics, and notions at prices consistently below most area retail fabric outlets. The fabric is neatly arranged for easy browsing. Careful shopping will uncover excellent bargains, often on imported or specialty fabric, but care should be taken to compare the quality of clothing fabrics before buying. Upholstery and drapery fabrics will be specially ordered at the regular prices. Free upholstery classes were available at the Tigard store when we visited. Each outlet organizes different classes and all are free.

Coupons clipped from the daily newspapers allow a 50% discount on patterns every month, and discounts of 10% are available to area junior and senior high school students.

DISCOUNT FABRICS WAREHOUSE STORE

4370 N.E. Halsey   288-9343
Hours: M-Sat. 10-5   VISA, MC, checks
Handicapped access: one step

Flawed fabrics which are not sold in other Discount Fabric stores are accumulated here. Some have drastic flaws, so keep a sharp eye out. However, these fabrics are at least 50% off retail, so small jobs which can be cut from the fabric around the flaw may be worth considering.

FABRIC WHOLESALERS

1928 N.E. 42nd   281-1033
Hours: M-F 9:30-9, Sat. 10-6, Sun. 12-6   VISA, MC, checks
Handicapped access: yes

Other locations:

335 N.E. 122nd Ave.	252-1885
10480 S.W. Beaverton-Hillsdale Hwy.	646-3181
15236 S.E. McLoughlin Blvd., Milw.	659-5715
1075 S.E. Baseline Rd., Hillsboro	640-5826
340 Gresham Mall, Gresham	667-9042

The store has changed in the last few years from selling simply "discount" fabrics to stocking higher quality yardage at generally lower prices. Variety is extensive, and special 10% discounts are available on purchases of whole bolts or on sales of more than $50 for groups and schools. Wednesday and Thursday newspaper ads often carry coupons for 50% discounts on patterns, and several times a year, sales allow 20% off on all yardage.

HANCOCK'S FABRIC WAREHOUSE

4500 N.E. 122nd   252-0253
Hours: M-F 10-9, Sat. 10-6, Sun. 12-5   VISA, MC, checks
Handicapped access: yes

Located in the K-Mart Plaza, this full-line fabric store consistently sells fabrics at somewhat less than its average retail counterpart. Patterns are often advertised at 15% off retail, tables offer specially-selected bolts at 25%-50% off, and trims usually are lower priced. However, quality and variety are often also somewhat less, and careful selection is necessary to get comparable values.

JANTZEN, INC. FABRIC OUTLET

2012 N.E. Hoyt   238-5396
Hours: 2nd Sat. of each month 9-4:30   VISA, MC, checks
Handicapped access: yes

Once a month the Jantzen factory offers the public a chance to buy excess fabric used in its sportswear at slightly more than the factory paid for it. All fabrics used for clothing are usually in stock, and the best buys are in the swimwear fabrics – nylon lycras, knits, etc. – but zippers, linings, and other materials are also available at a savings.

Jantzen excesses are supplemented with coordinated fabrics from the same mills to allow purchasers the opportunity for one-stop fabric shopping. Special orders for team or school uniform sewing can be arranged with prices often dependent on the quantity of fabric needed. A telephone call will also add your name to a mailing list of sale dates.

JAYVEE BRAND, INC. FACTORY OUTLET

113 Foothills Rd., Lake Oswego   **636-9691**
Hours: M-F 9-4, 2nd & 4th Sat. 10-2   VISA, MC, checks
Handicapped access: 1st floor, yes; stairs to 2nd floor

We classified this factory outlet as a "real find." The only outlet for 5 U.S. Jayvee factories, this is the place to buy all those baby shower presents that can be so expensive. The first floor is stocked with obsolete and overstock "firsts" for only $1 more than the seconds, which are less than half the retail price. The stock represents the entire Jayvee line – bibs, plastic pants, besides the sleepwear.

The second floor is filled with excess material and remnants. Yardage is substantially less than similar fabrics in retail stores, and remnant pieces are 25% lower than the marked price. All fabrics are flame retardant non-cottons – brushed nylon, flannels, terry cloth, denims, polyester, velour. Sewing notions, including a wide variety of iron-on decals, are carried at low prices. Scrap bags of fabric pieces good for quilts were $2, and an interesting array of bins sold bibs and bonnets for 10¢ each. Partially sewn, pre-cut garments, abandoned because of a flaw, are 25¢ each or sold by the pound. A saleslady said some women buy a bunch, finish them at home, and sell them at garage sales and church bazaars.

MILL END RETAIL STORE

8300 S.E. McLoughlin Blvd.   **236-1234**
Hours: M-F 9:30-8:30, Sat. 9:30-6,   VISA, MC, checks
**   Sun. 11-6**
Handicapped access: yes

Originally the "mill ends" outlet for the old Oregon Woolen Mills, the store is still located in the old factory warehouse. However, it is probably now the most complete sewing center in the Portland area and has 2 big secrets for bargain hunters: a mailing list (for walk-in customers only) which invites customers to several 25%-off sales a year (that's 25% off everything in the store including sewing machines!) and a "back room" where cut pieces of almost every fabric imaginable are sold at a discount, some sold by the pound!

Besides stocking the ordinary clothing fabrics, Mill End includes upholstery and drapery fabrics, rugs, carpeting, craft supplies, yarn, foam pads, and pillows. Do-it-yourself hints are hung about the store. Discounts of 10% on most merchandise are also available to senior citizens, schools, and professional seamstresses.

PENDLETON WOOLEN MILLS FACTORY OUTLET—See Clothing, Men's and Women's New

VAUGHAN BROS., INC.

1022 W. Burnside   **228-6485**
Hours: M-S 8-5   **Checks**
Handicapped access: 2 steps

Vaughan Bros. is "strictly a wholesale outlet" selling marine and awning canvases, industrial fabrics and hardware, upholstery fabrics, and convertible tops. BUT, we needed some canvas for a lawn chair, wandered in, and easily bought our 2½ yards for about 25% less than we had seen elsewhere. The secret is to know what you want and to bother them as little as possible. Browse elsewhere, but check Vaughan's before buying any specialty fabrics.

WESTERN MAJORETTE SUPPLY

7930 S.E. Stark   **235-3136**
Hours: M-Sat. 1-5   **VISA, MC, checks**
Handicapped access: stairway

This specialty fabric store caters to baton-twirlers, ice skaters, dancers (and occasionally to female impersonators!) in search of costume fabrics and trims not available in most retail outlets. Lamés, metallic chiffons, brocades, stretch satins, and flashy trims can be found at prices only slightly less than retail fabric stores, but the store offers buyers the opportunity to create their own disco costumes at a fraction of the price paid normally. A single strand of sequins sold for 15¢/yard, but a 1" band of rhinestones was $37/yard when we priced the merchandise. A remnant box offers savings on ends. Layaway can be arranged, and mail order sales are possible.

Flea Markets and Rummage Sales

Flea markets are just large garage sales held on someone else's property. Usually, the seller pays a fee to set up a table or booth, and the buyer, who might pay a small fee to enter, deals directly with each seller. Goods can range from clothing to cars and most items are sold as is. Persons who run flea market tables full time often buy items from liquidators or store close-outs and up the prices. Few accept returns, so if you have doubts about an item, make sure to talk over the possibility of returning it before buying it. Most sellers operate on a cash only basis. Dickering is a part of the buying process, so don't be afraid to make an offer.

BANNER FLEA MARKET

S.W. Tualatin Valley Hwy. (just east of Hillsboro)   640-6755
Hours: F, Sat., Sun. 12-5:30
Handicapped access: gravel lot

No admission is charged. A sales spot rents for $8 for the 3 days.

BONNIE'S RESALE

7912 S.W. Multnomah Blvd.   **No phone**
Hours: T-Sat. 10-5:30; F 12-5:30   **Checks**
Handicapped access: second floor, no elevator

On the 2nd floor of the 1914 Thomas Building in the Garden Home neighborhood is this one woman's try in the business world. Bonnie used to be a laboratory worker, but set up this consignment flea market business in 1978 more or less as a lark. She takes pretty much everything (except clothes), sets the prices according to how well she thinks an item will sell, and takes 40% of the profits. Signs say: "Make an offer; I might not," and dickering with the friendly, rosy-cheeked woman is fun. She does get a few antiques—a doily stretcher and a skate sharpener were both selling for under $1 the day we visited.

There were good buys on dishes, paperback books, vases, bamboo sun shades; many things seem to come from people who are moving and don't have the time to give their own garage sales.

HOLGATE (FARM) FLEA MARKET

S.E. 104th & Holgate   **760-8346**
Hours: Sat., Sun. 9-5
Handicapped access: yes

A 25¢ admission fee is asked of everyone over 12 years of age. Sales tables rent for $6 a day.

MEMORIAL COLISEUM FLEA MARKET

1401 N. Wheeler   **246-9996**
Hours: Sun. 10-4:30
Handicapped access: yes

Admission of 50¢ is asked. Tables must be rented at least a month in advance because of the high demand for space at this flea market. Call Don for more information.

SANDY BARR'S FLEA MARKET

8725 N. Chautauqua   **283-9565**
Handicapped access: 3 floors, no elevator

An admission charge of 50¢ is asked. A sales table can be rented for $6 a day.

SPRINGER'S FLEA MARKET

18300 S.E. Ritchie Rd., Gresham   **665-3568**
Hours: Sat.-Sun. 9:30-5
Handicapped access: yes

A 25¢ admission charge is asked. Tables rent for $15 for the 2 days.

CATLIN GABEL RUMMAGE SALE

Memorial Coliseum   **297-1894**
Hours: Th-Sat. 9-9   **VISA, MC, checks**
Handicapped access: yes

One of the oldest and largest rummage sales in Portland, the
Catlin Gabel sale is as much an event as a place to find bargains. Held each year during the last week in October or the
first in November, the sale attracts thousands of people and a
plethora of merchandise. Bill Walton's couch (custom made and
very long) sold in both the 1978 and 1979 sales – the first buyers
must have gotten more than they had bargained for. Six cars
were donated for the 1979 sale, too.

The essence of good rummage sale-ing was overheard from
one man buying an unidentified piece of metal with spikes and
two handles: "I don't know what it is, but it looks useful, and I
think I need it." Shoes are priced at about 5% of retail value; a
friend of ours has stocked his closet with $340-worth of shoes
for $26 over the last 3 years. Another friend buys many of her
books of French literature here. No admission fee is charged,
but the Coliseum gets its $1 for parking, although street park-
ing is available nearby.

TRINITY EPISCOPAL CHURCH RUMMAGE SALE

147 N.W. 9th   **222-9811**
Hours: W 11-4, Th-F 10-4   **Checks**
Handicapped access: 4 steps

One of the largest charitable rummage sales in Portland,
Trinity Episcopal's sale is famous for its quality merchandise.
Held the first week in October since 1939, the sale includes all
sorts of items from clothing to couches. Most of the clothing is
used, but many local retailers donate clothing (some with minor
flaws) that sells for low, low prices. Linens, sportswear, appliances, furniture, indeed anything that is donated, is put on
sale. In 1979 Portlanders carted off $25,000 in merchandise.

Food

(Also see Liquidators)

Bakery Goods

FRANZ BAKERY

10840 S.W. Cascade, Tigard	639-6806
Hours: M-F 9-6, Sat. 9-5	Checks
Handicapped access: yes	
Other locations:	
340 N.E. 11th	232-2191
11540 S.E. Foster Rd.	761-2412
331 N. Main, Gresham	665-2152

Franz Bakery outlets sell all day-old products at about 50% off. Breads of all kinds were selling 2 loaves for $1; hamburger and hot dog buns, 2 packages for 75¢ the day we visited. Fresh donuts sold for 50% less than in grocery stores, and day-old donuts for 10¢ less than that. Foodstamps are accepted.

LANGENDORF BREAD BOX

4926 S.E. Division	236-3660
Hours: M-F 9-5:30, Sat. 9-5	Checks
Handicapped access: yes	
Other locations:	
14510 S.E. Stark	254-5476
16585 S.E. McLoughlin Blvd.	659-5722

The entire Langendorf product line is sold here either day-old or fresh. Fresh products are usually discounted 10¢ off the retail price; savings are more substantial on day-old merchandise. Senior citizens may request a special discount coupon which entitles them to $2 of free merchandise after purchases of $30 are made.

MARSHALL'S DONUTS

11724 S.E. Division	761-2131
Hours: M-F midnight-8 a.m.	Checks
Handicapped access: yes	

If you order a dozen of any of the 15 varieties of Marshall's wholesale donuts 24 hours in advance, it will cost you $1.50. That's 30% less than found in most donut places. If you just stop by, the price jumps to $2.40. The management will take orders during the day, but pickup times are during working hours, which start at midnight. Get up early and get your donuts at wholesale prices.

OROWEAT BAKERY THRIFT STORE

10750 S.W. 5th, Bvrt.	643-5541
Hours: M-Sat. 9-6	Checks
Handicapped access: stairs	
Other locations:	
14750 S.W. Boones Ferry Rd.	635-3796
8303 S.E. Woodstock	774-5077
1100 S.E. 199th, Gresham	666-3845

The thrift store offers considerable savings on all Oroweat specialty bread products and has a continuous supply of the wide variety offered by Oroweat in retail outlets. Party hors d'oeuvres are made less expensively if the small rounds of French or rye bread are purchased here. Specialty breads such as Branola or Raisin Nut sell for about a 25% discount day-old; English muffins are 30% less and large bags of "seconds" are even cheaper, although hard to make "pop" out of a toaster. Pastries and cookies are brought fresh daily to the thrift store and sell at a discount. Store personnel appreciate customers bringing their own bags. Hours and handicapped access vary between stores, so a call before visiting will assure a successful trip. Food stamps are accepted.

PIERRE'S FRENCH BAKERY

700 S.E. Clay	233-8871
Hours: M-Sat. 9:30-6	Checks
Handicapped access: step	

Many of Portland's finest restaurants serve Pierre's French

bread and rolls, and some people say they are the best in town. The bakery sells the day-old French bread and its rolls, rye bread, and sliced breads for ½ off the fresh price.

WONDERBREAD BAKERY THRIFT SHOP

115 N. Cook   **282-7506**
Hours: M-Sat. 9-6   **Checks**
Handicapped access: yes

Want to buy a cheap Twinkie? Nothing in the large, well-stocked store has been there longer than 3 days, and prices are marked further down each day. A full line of Wonderbread bakery products is available plus some other items which are not priced lower, but are carried for shoppers' convenience. A 10¢-off coupon comes in each package, and special coupon cards worth $1.50 are given after $27-worth of merchandise has been purchased. Senior citizens get an automatic 10% discount, and food stamps are accepted.

Canneries

CORNELL'S CUSTOM CANNING

5001 N.E. 82nd   **252-9762**
Hours: April-Oct. varying hours   **Checks**
Handicapped access: yes, but awkward inside

Do it the clean, easy, and safe way, and do it the way you want it. That's the idea behind the only custom vegetable canning house in town. Bring in vegetables, tomato juice, fish – whatever – use their sinks, clean it, pack it in the cans, and Cornell's will do the hot work for you. Prices are very reasonable, and you can decide how much sugar and salt you want. They also can fish at the same price as Tony's Fish Market. Call first because hours vary with the season.

TONY'S FISH MARKET

14th & Washington, Oregon City   **656-7512**
Hours: M-Sat. 9-6   **Checks**
Handicapped access: curb
Other location:
12615 S.E. McLoughlin Blvd.   **654-0196**

At the price of smoked salmon these days, it's best to catch

your own and bring it to a custom canner. Tony's cans for
½-lb./50¢, 1-lb./60¢. Smoking and canning are 80¢ and $1.10
for the ½-lb. and lb., respectively. Smoking only is 50¢/lb. All
prices will probably go up a bit each year; these were 1979
prices.

Nuts, Candy, Party Food

GENERAL AMERICAN THEATRE SUPPLY CO.—
See Paper Goods

HOODY CORPORATION

5555 S.W. 107th, Bvrt.   646-0555
Hours: M-F 8-5, Sat. 8-2   Checks
Handicapped access: 6 steps

Having a party? Get the mixed nuts at Hoody's factory outlet. If you can handle the large quantities, you can save a bundle. Cashews, almonds, Brazil nuts, peanuts, filberts, maca-
damia, and pistachio nuts are all available, as well as peanut
butter and jams. Prices are based on case lots, and a 10¢/lb.
surcharge is added when buying less than a case. The minimum
sold is usually 10 lbs. of one thing. The 6 lb. cans of peanut butter are about $1 less per can than at grocery stores, when a
case of 6 is bought. Prices are especially good for the small
pieces of cashews, pecans, and almonds used in baking. The nut
sweepings from the floors are sold for bird feed for 30¢ a
pound—often no more expensive than wild bird seed in the
store, and certainly a gourmet treat for the birds! Empty plastic containers, about ½-gallon in size, sell for 25¢ each.

POPPERS SUPPLY—See Paper Goods

SEA FRESH COMPANY

3303 S.E. 20th   234-6872
Hours: M-F 8-5   Checks
Handicapped access: yes

This wholesale distributor of tavern foods—the pepperoni
sticks, beer sausage, nuts, and popcorn—sells to the public for
the same price as to his tavern customers. Though not quite as
cheap as others for already-popped popcorn, it is still lower

than retail food stores. Spanish peanuts can be bought here by the pound for about 40% less than at grocery stores, and all items are available for sale in small quantities.

VAN DUYN'S CANDY FACTORY STORE

739 N.E. Broadway   **287-1143**
Hours: M-Sat. 9-5:30   **VISA, MC, checks**
Handicapped access: yes

Whatever irregular chocolates Van Duyn's makes – usually the dipping hasn't covered the interior – as well as underweight boxes and some outdated candies are sold at the main store for savings of up to 40% off the regular retail price. Seasonally wrapped packages are also sold at a discount.

Produce

COMELLA & SON, INC.

6959 S.W. Garden Home Rd.   **245-5033**
Hours: M-Sat. 9-7, Sun. 10-5:30   **Checks**
Handicapped access: yes

Frank Comella moved to this Southwest location from a nearby shopping center, fulfilling his life-long dream of owning a produce and flower market run in the "Produce Row" tradition of Portland. He, his wife, son and daughter operate a friendly market where sampling is encouraged and lessons in the use or cleaning of fruit and vegetables are available for the asking. Variety is always extensive and prices usually significantly lower than in full-line groceries. Produce can be purchased in bulk for greater savings. Candy, bread, milk, Nancy's yogurt and eggs are kept on hand.

CORNO AND SON

711 S.E. Union Ave.   **232-3157**
Hours: M-Sat. 7-9, Sun. 8-7   **Checks**
Handicapped access: curb

When you say produce, everyone says "Corno's." In the old Italian produce warehouse section of Portland near the river, Corno's has the best quality, the most variety, and best prices and atmosphere around. The day in September we visited to check prices, we found 5 kinds of apple, 4 kinds of hot pepper, 3 kinds of carrots . . . ! We, who always buy bulk grains in food co-ops, were surprised to find that Corno's undersold them all on bulk whole wheat flour and rolled oats, and equalled the oriental groceries on bulk rice prices. They don't, however, beat the co-op prices on bulk spices. No. 10 cans of jam and peanut butter were the cheapest we found, except at the Hoody factory outlet. Buying canned foods in case lots will save another 5% on the Corno retail price. Frequent specials on produce also offer fantastic bargains – like a case of 12 very ripe pineapples for 98¢ or 50 lbs. of white onions for $1.49!

FARM PRODUCE GUIDE

Extension Services:
   Multnomah County: 1633 S.W. Park, 229-4841
   Washington County: 2448 S.W. Tualatin-Valley Hwy.,
      Bvrt., 648-8706
   Clackamas County: 256 Warner Milne Rd.,
      Oregon City, 655-8634

Going out to the farm to pick or buy your own produce is more than just a way to save money: it's recreation, and the assurance that you are getting the freshest possible food. It's also the perfect weekend activity for a family – get those kids out to the farm to learn that peaches don't grow in a crate and eggplants aren't laid by chickens. Without the middleman adding his percentage, most produce, especially the "u-pick" variety, is less expensive than in grocery stores and roadside stands. County extension agents in the Portland area publish a Farm Fresh Foods Guide each year with a description of the produce and a map of the location of some 50 participating farms. They will also provide a dial-an-answer service for food preservation tips from April through September. A catalog of tapes will be mailed on request. A home economist is also available on a food preservation "hot line" from 8:30-4:30 during the summer months.

GLEANING

   Low income, elderly, and handicapped people can receive free produce by gleaning fields in which the produce cannot be economically harvested. Strawberries, cucumbers, zucchini, broccoli, cabbage, corn, and tomatoes have all been available in summers past. Gleaners must provide their own containers and transportation, and must pick extra poundage for the elderly and handicapped who cannot get to the fields.

Gleaning coordinators in the Portland area are:

Portland Action Committees Together (PACT),
    2705 S.E. Milwaukie
Multnomah County Community Action Agency
    (MCCAA), 4420 S.E. 64th
Food Bank, 718 W. Burnside
North Community Action Council, 6965 N. Fessenden
Albina Action Center, 707 N.E. Knott
Washington County Community Action Organization,
    245 S.E. 2nd, Hillsboro
Clackamas County Community Action Agency,
    825 Portland, Gladstone
Community Action Team of Columbia County,
    Scappoose

SHERIDAN FRUIT CO.

409 S.E. Union   **235-9353**
Hours: M-Th, Sat. 7-8, F 7-9, Sun. 9-6   **Checks**
Handicapped access: yes

After Corno's, Sheridan Fruit Co. is the best known in town for quality produce and fair prices – the kind of place you just know you'll find some gooseberries. The store has recently expanded its bulk-size area to include a vast array of No. 10 cans of peanut butter, preserves, nuts, bulk rice, flour, and canned goods. Prices are a little higher on some goods than at Corno's, but the store isn't usually as crowded. They will also give discounts on volume buying. One salesman said buying in lots of 20 lbs. of fresh vegetables can bring a 10% discount. Check the wholesale list at the front counter to negotiate a price on canned goods – 5%-10% savings, reportedly.

Oriental Food Stores

We have always done some food shopping at the oriental

store in our neighborhood because (even before we started this book) it didn't make sense to buy rice by the 2 lb. box or soy sauce by the 16-oz. bottle. Neither spoil, and immense savings are available for buying in bulk. Additionally, the stocks of somewhat "uncommon" foods like ginger root or bok choy are much fresher than in a full-line American grocery, since the clientele assures more frequent re-stocking.

The stores listed below serve Portland's demand for foods from China, Japan, the Philippines, Thailand, Korea, Vietnam, and in some cases the Arab countries. Many have an oriental specialty, all carry short grain rice in 25-, 50-, and 100-lb. bags (most have long grain, too), all have a variety of soy sauces (some in bulk) and oils for use in either American or oriental cooking. Most also stock the fresh vegetables necessary for many oriental dishes, which are hard to find in most American groceries.

The day we checked, prices on most items were less than those same items in an American grocery but did vary from store to store. A phone call to the stores nearest you before stocking up might save you a few additional cents.

Several of the stores carry extensive stocks of oriental cookware (woks we found an exceptional buy), serving dishes, and gift items. For higher quality at usually lower prices, shopping for these things should begin at an oriental grocery.

ANZEN IMPORTS

736 N.E. Union   **233-5111**
Hours: M-Sat. 9-6:30, Sun. 12-5   **Checks**
Handicapped access: 3 steps

One of Portland's largest oriental groceries, Anzen carries mainly Japanese and Hawaiian foods. Half the store is dedicated to oriental gifts, serving dishes, and cookware, and the grocery half offers a large selection of fresh, frozen, dried, and canned foods. Fresh fish is always available, and the fresh vegetables were of good quality. Fresh sushi pastry is available every day except Sunday and Monday.

DAE HAN ORIENTAL FOODS AND GIFTS

9970 S.W. Beaverton-Hillsdale Hwy.   **646-7127**
Hours: M-Sat. 10-7, Sun. 1-7   **Checks**
Handicapped access: curb

If you're not used to shopping "oriental," this store is truly an experience the first time you walk in! It has an amazing variety of foods, cookware, and gifts from most countries in the Orient, all displayed pleasantly in a cheerful open setting. Fresh, frozen, canned, and dried foods are stocked all year, with special sales on fresh meats 3 or 4 times a year. Food stamps are *not* accepted.

EBISU IMPORTS

1435 S.E. Hawthorne Blvd.   **233-1416**
Hours: M-Sat. 9-7, Sun. 12-5   **VISA, MC, checks**
Handicapped access: yes

Ebisu carries mainly foods and gifts of the Japanese culture, but maintains adequate stocks of Chinese foods, oils, and sauces. Fresh vegetables are always available, and fish can be had dried, frozen, or fresh. Fridays and Saturdays offer freshly-made sushi pastry. Long and short grain rice is available in bulk quantities.

FONG CHONG GROCERY

403 N.W. 5th   **223-1777**
Hours: M-Sat. 8:30-6   **Checks**
Handicapped access: one step

Fong Chong is the largest of Portland's oriental groceries and supplies many of the smaller ones in the state. Prices here were as low or lower than we found in other oriental stores, and many grades of both long and short grain rice were sold in bulk. Full lines of canned, dried, and frozen foods were displayed, and the fresh vegetables were the best seen anywhere. They also offer barbecued meats.

KOREAN FOODS AND GIFTS (SHIN SHIN MARKET)

2001 S.E. Stark   **232-9111**
Hours: M-F 8-7, Sat. 9-7, Sun. 10:30-7   **Checks**
Handicapped access: steps inside

Run by the Shin Shin family for the last 10 years in a southeast Portland neighborhood, the market serves as both the corner "Mom 'n Pop" and an oriental grocery. The variety of oriental foods was not as extensive as in some other groceries but included all the essentials and fresh vegetables. Their specialties are homemade kim chee, bulk salted and dried shrimp, and a mixture of canned spiced vegetables packed at the store. Food stamps are accepted.

MANILA IMPORTS

116 N.E. 28th   **233-6830**
Hours: 10-6 every day   **Checks**
Handicapped access: yes

One of the smaller groceries, Manila has been at this location for 5 years, but may soon be moving because its building is for sale. The day we visited, stocks were only about half of what we found elsewhere, but the owner assured us that was a temporary phenomenon. Fresh vegetables arrive from Hawaii each weekend, and the foods include those of the Philippines, Arab countries, Thailand, Spain, and China.

MEKONG ORIENTAL FOODS AND GIFTS

1805 N.E. 39th   **281-7108**
Hours: 10-8 every day   **Checks**
Handicapped access: curb

The fresh vegetables and ginger root impressed us most in this oriental grocery. Canned, frozen, dried, and fresh foods and meats from Vietnam, Thailand, Japan, and China are always stocked, and both short and long grain rice is available in bulk. A large selection of oriental music on tapes was displayed behind the counter. Teas in gift cans and some oriental cookware was for sale. Food stamps are accepted.

THE SHANGHAI COMPANY

2865 S.E. Division   **235-2525**
Hours: M-F 8-4   **Checks**
Handicapped access: steep hill

The cheapest fortune cookies in town are sold here by 10-lb. lots. Bean sprouts were also cheaper than we found in the oriental grocery stores. The manufacturer also sells wonton wrappers and fried noodles at less than retail prices. Most of their business is to other grocery stores, but they will readily sell to the general public.

TUCK LUNG GROCERY

140 N.W. 4th	**223-1090**
Hours: M-F 9-7, Sat. 9-6:30, Sun. 10-5	**Checks**
Handicapped access: yes	

One of Portland's most well-established oriental groceries and restaurants, Tuck Lung has a large stock of dried, frozen, canned, and fresh oriental foods at prices sometimes a little higher than other oriental groceries. Their stocks of cookware and gifts were not as extensive as we found in other stores, however. Their specialties are barbecued meats – hanging for your inspection and choice – and Peking duck, neither of which can be found in other groceries. Food stamps are accepted.

Food Co-ops and Natural Food Stores

Natural food stores and food co-ops should not be considered the exclusive domain of the "counter culture." The idea that most food items need individual wrapping and pricing is now growing obsolete for more and more of America's food buyers. Shoppers at these stores bring their own bags and jars, thereby saving our world's dwindling resources as well as their own dollars. Pricing and bagging the food yourself reduces overhead that is added to the food prices of grocery stores. The stores listed here cater to vegetarian tastes, specializing in whole grains, a variety of nut butters, farm-direct dairy products and vegetables – both organically and non-organically grown. The best prices can be found on spices, with bulk grains a close second. Buying unpackaged spices from air-tight jars saves an incredible amount of money, sometimes as much as 80%, and usually at least 50% of the prices found on the bottled, store varieties. We did notice, however, that garlic salt was cheaper in the grocery stores, for some unexplained reason. Savings are even greater at food co-ops where shoppers can pay a membership fee and work a few hours a month for the extra discounts. Senior citizens usually receive that same discount without working. Besides the money-saving potential found, we like to shop at these stores for the unhurried and friendly atmosphere and the opportunity to re-use old containers.

FOOD FOR THOUGHT

106 Molalla, Oregon City   **657-0071**

Hours: M-Sat. 10-6:30   **Checks**
Handicapped access: yes

Membership is $3, and 3 hours of work per month brings a
10% discount on their prices. Twelve hours of work gives a
20% discount. Senior citizens get an automatic 5% discount.

FOOD FRONT

2635 N.W. Thurman   222-5658
Hours: M-Sat. 11-7   **Checks**
Handicapped access: 4 steps

Food Front will be building a new store next door. Membership fee is $4, one-time only, with an 18% discount for 3 hours
of work a month. Senior citizens over 65 get an automatic discount.

MILK AND HONEY FOOD CO-OP

18930 S.W. Boones Ferry Rd., Tualatin   638-6227
Hours: M 10-8, T-Sat. 10-6   **Checks**
Handicapped access: yes

Two hours of work a month give a 5% discount. Members of
other co-ops and senior citizens have an automatic discount
here.

PEOPLE'S FOOD STORE

3029 S.E. 21st   232-9051
Hours: M, F 10-8; T, Th, Sat. 10-7; Sun. 1-5   **Checks**
Handicapped access: yes

The oldest co-op in town, People's works on a 17% mark-up
over cost. Members who pay a $1 fee and senior citizens receive
13% discounts. Special orders of natural foods in bulk, from the
Starflower Company in Eugene, can be made through the co-
op on Wednesdays and picked up on Fridays at a 15% discount
from the regular co-op prices.

SENIOR CITIZEN GROCERY

4707 N. Lombard   285-4141
Hours: M-Sat. 9-5   **Checks**
Handicapped access: curb

Though not really a food co-op, this grocery store is staffed only by volunteers and limits its customers to those over 60 years of age. The non-profit organization prices everything at just 10% over wholesale, thus cutting a hefty percentage off normal retail prices. There is no fresh meat or produce, but canned goods and non-perishables are at great prices and in good variety. John Piacentini, owner of the Plaid Pantry stores, is credited with starting the unique grocery several years ago with a donation of $20,000-worth of foodstuffs and free use of a former market.

KING HARVEST NATURAL FOODS

2348 S.E. Ankeny   235-5358
Hours: M-F 9:30-7, Sat. 9:30-6   Checks
Handicapped access: yes

NATURE'S FOOD AND TOOL

5909 S.W. Corbett   244-8996
Hours: M-Sat. 10-8   Checks
Handicapped access: two steps
Other location:
3437 N.E. 24th   288-3414

ROSS ISLAND GROCERY

3338 S.W. Corbett   227-4531
Hours: Every day 9-9   Checks
Handicapped access: yes

Wine and Beer Wholesalers

Oregon State liquor law allows wholesalers to sell to the public with only the restriction of a minimum 5-gallon sale. We have visited most of the wholesalers listed and found them pleasant, knowledgeable, and willing to help the buyer choose wines or beers to his liking. All wholesalers sell domestic and imported wines, but specialize as to vineyard, importer, or country. Some sell domestic and imported beers as well. Some will allow the mixing of cases. The definition of "5-gallon" did vary from wholesaler to wholesaler, we found, but all made possible savings of from 30%-50% on wines, beers, and champagnes.

After you've discovered which wine or beer you'll want to buy by the case, check around for the lowest prices, as they do vary. We recently saved about 35% on 7 cases of Asti Spumante (purchased with friends!) at McClaskey's.

AL GUISTI

66 S.E. Morrison   **232-4124**
Hours: M-F 9-4   **Cash only**
Handicapped access: stairs

They carry imported, California and Oregon wines and no beer. The minimum puchase is 3 cases, and mixing of cases is not allowed.

COLUMBIA DISTRIBUTING COMPANY

2448 N.W. 28th   **227-6506**
Hours: M-F 9-4   **Cash only**
Handicapped access: yes
Other location:
Maletis, Inc., 5580 S.W.107th, Bvrt.   **644-1900**

They sell imported, California, and Oregon wines and domestic and imported beers. The minimum wine purchase is 2½ cases, of beer it's 3 cases. They will not allow mixing of cases.

CROWN CENTURY WINE

16444 S.W. 72nd   **620-5777**
Hours: M-F 9-5, by appt. Sat. & Sun.   **Checks**
Handicapped access: 4 steps

They carry imported, California and Oregon wines and will soon have imported beers. The minimum purchase of wines is 2 cases and 2 bottles, and mixing of cases is allowed.

GAM AND COMPANY

2443 S.E. 4th   **232-1178**
Hours: M-F 8-5   **Cash only**
Handicapped access: curb

They carry imported and California wines and imported and domestic beers. The minimum wine purchase is 2 cases and 2 bottles, of beer it's 3 cases. They will allow mixing of half-cases.

LAFRANCE WINE COMPANY

222 S.E. Alder   **233-8787**
Hours: M-F 8:30-5:30, Sat. 10-12   **Checks**
Handicapped access: yes

They carry imported, California, and Oregon wines and imported beers. The minimum purchase is 3 cases, either beer or wine, and they do not allow the mixing of cases of fifths.

McCLASKEY'S WINE DISTRIBUTORS

930 N.W. 14th   **224-3150**
Hours: M-F 8:30-5:30   **Checks**
Handicapped access: yes

They carry imported, California, and Oregon wines, but no beer. The minimum purchase is 2½ cases, and they will allow mixing of cases as low as 3 bottles of one kind.

ROBERTI'S HOUSE OF WINES

808 S.E. Alder   **234-7551**
Hours: M-F 8-5   **Checks**
Handicapped access: 6 steps

They sell imported, California, and Oregon wines and imported beers. The minimum purchase of wine is 2½ cases, of beer it's 3 cases. They will allow the splitting of cases into half-cases of different kinds of wines.

SPEAR BEVERAGE COMPANY

5825 N.E. Skyport Way   **288-8831**
Hours: M-F 8-5   **Checks**
Handicapped access: yes

They carry imported and California wines and domestic and imported beers. The minimum wine purchase is 2 cases and 2 bottles, and 3 cases for beer. They will allow mixing by the case, i.e. you may buy one case of 2 different wines.

Miscellaneous

DICKINSON FAMILY PANTRY

7325 S.W. Bonita Rd., Tigard   **639-4117**
Hours: M-F 8-4:30   **VISA, MC, checks**
Handicapped access: 6 steps

After 81 years in the mail order preserve business, the Dickinson Family is known nationwide. Their factory is in Tigard, with a small retail outlet next door. In fact, to get help, you have to walk into the work area and ask. But don't hesitate, the savings are worth the experience. In buying the delicious blackberry preserves, orange marmalade, boysenberry jelly or syrup, loganberry jelly, Concord grape, currant, gooseberry, or plum preserves at this factory outlet, you can save almost ½ the price you would pay in a downtown retail store. Though the Dickinson family doesn't own the operation anymore, the family tradition of quality has been preserved.

DISCOUNT CANNED GOODS

13500 S.E. Powell Blvd.   **760-8425**
Hours: M-Sat. 10:30-5:30   **Checks**
Handicapped access: yes

Case and ½-case quantities of damaged Walla Walla canned fruits and vegetables are sold at wholesale price or below. The cans are usually dented through shipment but are all federally inspected for quality.

THE POP SHOPPE

1313 S.E. 82nd   **255-9794**
Hours: M-F 10-7, Sat-Sun. 10-6   **VISA, MC, checks**
Handicapped access: yes
Other locations:
See the Yellow Pages—Beverages for 15 dealers

Pop in 24 flavors can be bought by the case for about half what other brands cost in grocery stores. Only cases of 24 10-oz. bottles or 24 quart bottles are available, and a $4 bottle deposit is charged on the first purchase. Most of the stores are located with gas stations and have their own hours. Listed is the bottling plant and main store.

PRAIRIE MARKET

8950 S.W. Commercial, Tigard   **639-6334**
Hours: M-W 9-7, Th-F 9-8, Sat. 9-5:30   **Checks**
Handicapped access: yes
Other locations: See Yellow Pages-Alphabetical listings

Prairie Market has reduced shopping to the basics: items are left in cases, not marked, and stacked in a warehouse with few amenities. The idea is to pay a 50¢ membership fee, grab a cart and grease pencil, and go shopping. Prices are marked on the shelves per individual item and per case. Take your calculator to figure out the savings on the case prices; we found it usually didn't amount to more than 10¢-60¢. However, their prices were below those of most grocery stores on individual items. Even the paperback books located at the check-out stands were marked down 10%.

THE TACO SHAK

17466 S.E. Division   **761-4234**
Hours: M-Sat. 9-5   **Checks**
Handicapped access: yes

For Mexican food lovers, this is the place to get fresh tortillas and tamales. Two sizes of corn tortillas are sold by the dozen at the lowest price we found anywhere. Freshly-ground masa to make your own tamales is sold, as are the already-prepared tamales. Call ahead to place your order; the door is in the back.

WAREMART

4750 S.W. Western, Bvrt.   **No phone**
Hours: M-Sat. 8-11, Sun. 9-10   **Checks**
Handicapped access: yes

Though its prices are not quite as low as those at a similar warehouse food distributor, Waremart is open longer hours and has several time-saving shopping helps. Prices are still good, especially the weekly green tag specials. No membership fee is charged, and the new computer system has eliminated the need for customers to mark each item. The prices are marked on the shelves, and when the clerk runs the price code over the electric eye, the right price is automatically registered. No discount is given for buying by the case lot, but you do bag your own groceries.

Furniture, New and Used

(Also see Flea Markets, Liquidators,
Store Outlets, Thrift Shops)

Home Furnishings

FORENTCO

3103 N.E. Sandy Blvd.   **233-8622**
Hours: M-F 10-9, Sat. 10-5, Sun. 12-5   **VISA, MC, checks**
Handicapped access: service elevator to 2nd floor

Beginning as only a furniture rental company, Forentco management soon found they could sell returned rental merchandise, as well as new items of the same style merchandise they rented, for less than their competitors. Specializing in less expensive brands of home and office furniture and contemporary fiberboard, plastic, or chrome furnishings, the company sells their "rental returns" at less than the original manufacturer's cost, and new merchandise is marked up 20%-50% less than a normal retail markup. Brands carried are Easy Rest, DML, Allied, Lane, Douglas, Tempo, and Seeley. Good savings are available especially on Seeley mattresses because Forentco buys them in volumes up to 6,000 at a time and at 20%-30% less than the wholesale price to other retailers.

Both layaway and credit terms are available, as is delivery with a set charge. However, a "Preferred Customer" card allows a purchaser free delivery, home setup, special "closed door" sales, and other purchase incentives.

LEVITZ FURNITURE WAREHOUSE

13631 S.E. Johnson Rd., Milw.   **659-8431**
Hours: M-F 10-9, Sat. 10-6,   **Checks, Levitz credit card**
      Sun. 12-6
Handicapped access: yes

Levitz, of the famous "love it" ads, is worth the trip for comparison shopping just to see couches stacked 8 deep on 75-ft.

high warehouse shelves or the purring fork lifts extracting someone's choice from the top range of cardboard-covered furniture. Savings on name brand furniture and accessories like Burlington, Singer, Armstrong, Bassett, Lea, and Simmons are passed on to the purchaser by the manufacturer-to-warehouse-to-purchaser sales technique used by the company.

An extensive showroom attractively displays the contents of all the warehouse cartons for shopping and quality comparison. Floor samples are sold up to 30% off and an end-of-the-month sale offers savings of 50% on select items. An "as-is" store sells returned or damaged merchandise at half price, with the reason for discount clearly marked. (No refunds or exchanges are allowed on merchandise purchased "as is.") Layaway is available, and a significant amount can be saved by carrying merchandise home yourself.

MR. D AND SONS

8114 S.E. Division   **775-4124**
Hours: M-F 10-8, Sat. 10-6, Sun. 12-6   VISA, MC, checks
Handicapped access: curb

Furniture and carpets are advertised 20% below normal retail prices at this store. Bassett, American Drew, Virginia House, Allied, and Simmons are among the brands sold. A friend of ours compared hide-a-bed prices in Portland and found the best deal here. Delivery is free on an order of more than $200, and cash and carry prices are sometimes reduced on large items. The store will not guarantee any fabric, so if you are in doubt as to the quality of a certain fabric, make sure the manufacturer has a warranty on it. The store will special order fabric of the same grade for no extra charge.

MORCAMBE BAY CO. ANTIQUES

1314 N.W. Glisan   **233-0999**
Hours: Th-F 10-9; Sat., Sun., M 10-5   VISA, MC, checks
Handicapped access: 6 stairs

A monthly, 3-day sale features antique furniture and glassware from England on 3 floors (there is an elevator inside). Items can be previewed—with prices marked—on Thursday and Friday. Prices are firm on the first day of the sale, Saturday, but the company will accept "reasonable offers" on Sunday and Monday. The selection is often well picked over by Monday, but a friend of ours bought a table for $10 less than the asking price on the 3rd day. The sales are advertised in the daily papers, but ask to be put on the mailing list to receive announcements of each sale.

Unfinished Furniture

If your furniture budget is closer to wood veneer than solid oak, check the unfinished furniture stores. Though not inexpensive, they can save you about ⅓-½ the price of a fine solid wood piece of furniture. With a little advice, a few supplies, and a little practice you can make yourself just what you saw in the interior decorating magazine.

The places we visited had comparable selection and prices with items ranging from wine racks to bentwood rockers to filing cabinets. We even found some solid wood animal puzzles. Each store has a layaway plan and will deliver for a fee. All the stores offer advice on finishing, and many carry the supplies.

NATURAL FURNITURE

800 N.E. Broadway   284-0655
Hours: M-Th, Sat. 10-5:30, F 10-7,   VISA, MC, checks
          Sun. 12-5
Handicapped access: yes

STANTON UNFINISHED FURNITURE

1712 N.E. Sandy Blvd.   236-5216
Hours: M, F 10-9, T,W, Th, Sat. 10-5:30, VISA, MC, checks
          Sun. 11-5
Handicapped access: yes
Other locations:
10800 S.E. 82nd, Milw.   777-4311
10175 S.W. Beaverton-Hillsdale Highway, Bvrt.   644-7333

UNION FURNITURE

3590 S.E. Hawthorne Blvd.   231-0778
Hours: M-Th 9-6, F 9-8:30, Sat. 9-5,   VISA, MC, checks
          Sun. 12-4
Handicapped access: yes

Upstairs room has sales on one-of-a-kind which are marked down one-third of regular price. Cash only is accepted on sale items.

Office Furniture, New and Used

A-1 OFFICE FURNITURE

827 S.W. 2nd   223-2525
Hours: M-F 8-5, Sat. 8-12   Checks
Handicapped access: yes

Located in downtown Portland, A-1's Ben Wexler is a long-time merchandiser of used office equipment and furniture. He deals mainly in the cast-offs from government and private offices replacing their old office appointments with new. Those "cast-offs" often include solid oak desks, chairs, and filing cabinets, all at incredible savings to the searcher willing to do some refinishing. (The wonder of "real" wood is that it *can* be refinished, and the day we visited, no oak desk was higher than $250, all drawers in working order.)

Mr. Wexler buys everything left in offices after a move, and excellent buys can also be found on smaller office items such as vertical files, in-and-out baskets, posting tubs, chalk boards, ad infinitum. Collectors (if anyone does collect such memorabilia?) may even find something among the old, often original and unopened boxes of pencils, staples, pens, erasers, etc. Delivery is free in the downtown area, $5 to $10 outside of downtown. There is no warranty, but returns are allowed within the first 2 days.

D.C. WAX

219 S.W. Broadway   228-4313
Hours: M-F 8-5   VISA, MC, checks
Handicapped access: stairs to upstairs showroom

Located in an architecturally delightful building in downtown Portland, D.C. Wax caters mainly to large purchasers of new, usually metal office furniture, but will give any purchaser at least a 15% discount from catalog prices on new merchandise. That discount varies, however, up to 35% depending on the item and a buyer's persistence. If you know what you want, what you want to pay, and what others are selling for, you may be able to "cut some good deals" with the salesmen. All new merchandise comes with the manufacturer's warranty and delivery is available, either free or with a small charge.

Used metal office furniture is sold on the 2nd floor at prices based on condition. Prices are sometimes higher than for the less expensive lines of office furniture, but the quality may be higher on furniture in good condition. No warranty is given on used furniture, and buyers should know what they are looking for (and at) before purchasing.

DISCOUNT OFFICE SUPPLIES — See Arts, Crafts, and Hobby Supplies

GRANTREE FURNITURE RENTAL

601 N.E. Union   **287-3156**
Hours: M-F 9-7, Sat. 10-5   **VISA, MC, checks**
Handicapped access: yes

Grantree sells new and rental return office furniture from this warehouse-showroom store. They carry the usual lines of metal and steel office furniture, and have no wooden pieces. Accessories can be purchased, too. The prices vary on rental returns based on the condition of the piece. Lease terms are available if you don't wish to buy; delivery is charged according to the price of the item; warranties are only on the new furniture.

THE MART

2205 E. Burnside   **233-7665**
Hours: M-F 8:30-5:30, Sat. 10-4   **VISA, MC**
Handicapped access: yes

The MART discount office furniture store sells to the public, but has some of the best office furniture prices because they also handle many of the government office contracts in the area. All their furniture and accessories are new, none are freight damaged, and most are of the metal and steel variety. Some more expensive wooden executive office furniture is also sold, which might fit well in homes. Brands carried are Anderson, Art Steel, Wilshire, HON, Decentury, and discounts will be given for large orders. Delivery has a charge.

Grooming

Beauty and barber colleges offer savings well worth the experiment of letting a student perfect his skill with you as the model. Instructors carefully watch and inspect the work, and the main drawback is the bit more time the appointment may take because of the student's inexperience. We priced 3 of the more common hair care items – a shampoo and set, a permanent, and a haircut – and found them universally less than ½ the price charged by most beauty salons. Each college offers the same services and up-to-date styles found in beauty salons, although the experience of the staff is not, of course, the same. All conduct business in a professional manner. Most schools will take walk-in customers before 3 p.m., but prefer appointments, which can be made the same day. Most have special senior citizen days and discounts.

BEAU MONDE COLLEGE OF BEAUTY

821 S.W. 11th   226-7355
Hours: T-F 9:30-3:30, Sat. 8:30-3:30   VISA, MC, checks
Handicapped access: yes

Full beauty services are available for men and women, and walk-ins are possible. For those busy people who only want their hair shampooed after work, that is possible here for only $1.25. Senior citizen days are Tuesday, Wednesday, and Thursday (for those over 62), and a special price list is in effect offering a discount somewhat smaller than at other schools in the area.

COLLEGE OF BEAUTY

3925 N.E. Hancock   282-0985
Hours: T-F 9-3:30, Sat. 8-3:30   Checks
Handicapped access: yes

They offer the full line of hair care services for men and women. Walk-in appointments are possible, but the preference is for appointments made by 3:30 of the same day. Senior citizen days are Tuesday, Wednesday and Thursday (for anyone over 62), and provide a discount of 20% on all services.

COSMETOLOGY CAREERS UNLIMITED, INC.

1727 N.E. 40th   **288-6937**
Hours: T, W, F 9:30-5; Th 10:30-5   **VISA, MC, checks**
    Sat. 8:30-5
Handicapped access: yes

Full beauty services are available for men and women with appointments made at least a day in advance. Senior citizen days are Tuesday, Wednesday, and Thursday and prices of a shampoo and set and haircuts are discounted. Free color rinses are available those days for the senior citizens, too.

EXECUTIVE INSTITUTE OF HAIR DESIGN FOR MEN AND WOMEN

8138 S.E. Stark   **255-4774**
Hours: T-Sat. 9-5   **VISA, MC, checks**
Handicapped access: yes

A full line beauty parlor whose haircut price of $5 includes a shampoo and blow-dry. No appointments are taken after 4:45, and walk-ins are discouraged. Senior citizen days are Tuesday and Wednesday, when everything is 20% less.

MILWAUKIE BEAUTY SCHOOL

10574 S.E. 32nd, Milw.   **659-2834**
Hours: T-Sat. 8:30-5   **VISA, MC, checks**
Handicapped access: yes

Full service beauty shop for men and women. Appointments are best, but walk-ins can sometimes be fit into the schedule. Senior citizen days are Tuesday and Wednesday and offer a discount of 10% on all services.

MOLER BARBER COLLEGE

515 S.W. 3rd   **223-9818**
Hours: T-Sat. 8:30-5:30   **Cash only**
Handicapped access: yes

A wide variety of beauty care treatments are available to men here, although some women's haircuts are given. Shaves, beard trims, hair cuts and "styling," afros, and facials all are at a fraction of the price paid at most beauty salons. Appointments should be made, and there are no senior citizen discounts given.

MULTNOMAH COLLEGE OF HAIR DESIGN, INC.

12303 S.E. Division   761-5747
Hours: T-Sat. 8:30-5   Checks
Handicapped access: yes

Hair care services for men and women are offered, usually with appointment, but walk-ins are possible. Senior citizen days are Tuesday and Wednesday, with a 10% discount on all purchases.

PHAGAN'S SCHOOLS OF HAIR DESIGN

726 S.W. 4th   226-3891
Hours: T-Sat. 8:30-5   VISA, checks
Handicapped access: yes
Other locations:
10640 N.E. Halsey   255-8580
12750 S.W. Pacific Hwy., Tigard   639-6106

They offer beauty services to men and women and insist on appointments made usually one week in advance. They do, they admit, take some walk-in business, but to be sure of your appointment, make it! Senior citizens (over 60) receive discounts of 10% on all purchases any time.

UNIVERSITY BEAUTY COLLEGE

4790 N. Lombard   285-9271
Hours: T-Th 10-4:30, F 9-4:30, Sat. 8-4:30   Checks
Handicapped access: yes

They offer the full line of hair care services for men and women. No appointment is taken after 3:30, and Friday and Saturday are particularly busy. Senior citizens pay a one-time $3 membership for the "golden key" which allows them savings of 20% at any time.

Hardware

(Also see Catalog Discounters, Flea Markets,
Liquidators)

Interior Decorating

(Also see Building Materials, Fabrics)

AMERICAN FABRICS — See Fabrics

BEDSPREADS, ETC.

16097 S.E. McLoughlin Blvd.	654-9565
Hours: M-Sat. 10-6, F 10-9	VISA, MC, checks
Handicapped access: yes	

Lyn and Dale Williams are trying to take advantage of inflated department store prices and the whims of merchandising to make themselves some money while saving money for their customers. Their first quality bedspreads, linens, and pillows are all factory-direct and bought in volume lots. Adding these savings to the low overhead they maintain by avoiding a more expensive shopping center location across the street, they can save customers about 30% on the same merchandise found in other retail stores.

Cannon towels, Bates bedspreads, and Burlington sheets are only a few of the name brands in their extensive stock. These are not discontinued patterns, but ones that match linen to bedspread to towel. The owners will also special order from the manufacturer and pass a 15% savings on to the customer. No refunds are given, but exchanges can be made within 3 days of the purchase.

BITS AND PIECES

7119 S.E. Milwaukie	231-5076
Hours: M-Sat. 9:30-6, Sun. 12-5	VISA, MC, checks
Handicapped access: yes	

Other location:
1420 N.W. Lovejoy   **222-3847**

I. Layton Creations, a Northwest Portland bedspread and pillow manufacturer, sells its seconds and some first quality stock at these 2 outlets. (The factory outlet is not open on Sundays.) The stores do not have the usual "warehouse" atmosphere but rather the look and service of a retail department store.

First quality is sold in the "Finer Touch" rooms, and we found some bedspreads there for ½ the normal retail price. These were the same styles sold to major Portland retail department stores. The handwoven tasselled pillows made in India were less than ½ what they were selling for in those retail stores the day we checked prices. The seconds are well marked and usually are due to a dye flaw or crumpled batting. An additional 20% is taken off the price when a bedspread is bought with a matching headboard. This is also a great place to buy batting for soft sculpture and quiltmaking. Only credit or exchanges are allowed on returns.

CALICO CORNERS — See Fabrics

DISCOUNT WALLPAPER

10510 N.E. Halsey (off 106th)   **256-3400**
Hours: M-Sat. 10-6   **VISA, MC, checks**
Handicapped access: curb

The smallest discount here is an immediate 10% off on all current wallpaper book prices. For current wallpaper patterns sold from dealer's overstocks and limited to the quantity on hand (no special orders from the manufacturer's book), a 20% discount is offered. Greatest savings are on papers discontinued by the distributors, with savings of 50% off the book prices. These papers are also limited to the stock on hand. Over 200 patterns are continuously stocked, with names like Kinney, Wall Inc., Sinclair, Dunn Edwards, and Wall Products being the usual lines. Free demonstrations are given by members of this genial, family-run store staff, and a practice station is set up to let you make your first attempts on someone else's wall.

IMPERIAL PAINTS FACTORY STORE — See Building
Materials

J.C. PENNEY CUSTOM DRAPERY WORKROOM OUTLET

1720 S.E. 10th   **232-6174**
Hours: M-F 9-4   VISA, MC, checks, Penney credit card
Handicapped access: yes

Custom-made drapes here are 40%-60% off the original price, if you can find sizes that fit your windows. All the drapes, woven woods, and mini-blinds have been returned by customers dissatisfied with the color or design. And, if they don't fit your color scheme once you get them home, the Outlet will take them back. The largest selection is found in drapes; however, the variety changes with customers' whims.

STANDARD BRANDS PAINT CO. — See Building Materials

WALLPAPERS TO GO

15601 S.E. McLoughlin Blvd.   **654-3149**
Hours: M-F 10-9, Sat. 9-6, Sun. 12-5   VISA, MC, checks
Handicapped access: yes
Other location:
10205 S.W. Beaverton-Hillsdale Highway, Bvrt.   643-7523

If we are any judge of merchandising, our bet is that this store will revolutionize how wallpaper is sold — no dusty, cumbersome books that give you only a glimpse of 2 sq. ft. of paper cluttering their shelves! This wallpaper center displays every sample on a wall with a bin of rolls right next to it. Strolling up and down aisles gives an immediate overview of all papers, and on-hand stocks let you get your job started immediately. Papers are moderately priced and are available in the full range of vinyls, woven woods, flocked papers, etc. A bargain barrel is always full of discontinued patterns, and bundle lots are priced from 50%-80% off. For even more convenience, the store gives a full refund if you aren't satisfied after hanging 2 rolls, as long as you keep the receipt. Friendly salespeople will help you figure the amount needed and will divide double rolls without charge. Free paper hanging classes are held daily.

WAREHOUSE FLOORS

1235 S.E. Division   235-2128
Hours: M-Sat. 8:30-5:30 F 8:30-9   VISA, MC, checks
Handicapped access: yes

Strictly a cash-and-carry store, Warehouse Floors is a bare-bones operation with few amenities but great savings. Even contractors buy here because of the lower-than-wholesale prices. Some of the 700 rolls of linoleum and 600 rolls of carpet are discontinued or irregular patterns, but every piece can be examined in the store. The best buys are the factory over-stocks, prices varying according to what the owner paid for it and what he thinks he can get for it. The day we visited, several patterns of Congoleum were priced at $4.95/sq. yd. and were selling for $10/sq. yd. elsewhere! They do not install but will give advice if you want to tackle it yourself or will suggest the name of a professional installer. Not much Formica was stocked the day we visited, but the remnant bin was worth checking for the 10% extra savings. Refunds vary according to what and how much is returned.

Kitchen Supplies

(Also see Oriental Food Stores,
Flea Markets, Thrift Shops)

BASKIN-ROBBINS 31 ICE CREAM STORES

9206 S.W. Beaverton-Hillsdale Hwy.   297-3225
Hours: Sun.-Th 11-10; F-Sat. 11-11   Checks
Handicapped access: curb
Other locations:
See the Yellow Pages—Ice Cream Dealers

One of the best bargains at Dorothy Holt's Baskin-Robbins franchise is the plastic boxes with lids which transport strawberries for the ice cream sundaes. She saves these and gives them away to customers who use them for refrigerator storage or freezer containers. Made of very sturdy plastic, with tight-fitting lids, they are as good as any Tupperware product, but only come in pint sizes.

Mrs. Holt also saves and gives away free the 2-gallon ice cream containers made of cardboard with a metal bottom. Decorated with cloth, wine labels, or pretty pictures, they make wonderful storage bins or wastebaskets. There is, of course, a limited supply of these, and we didn't check all the Baskin-Robbins stores to see if they would keep their old containers. We bet, though, if you ask your neighborhood Baskin-Robbins owner, he or she will save them for you.

Liquidators

A-1 LIQUIDATORS

3614 S.E. Division
Hours: T-Sat. 9-5; day off varies
Handicapped access: yes

234-1041
Checks

Vern Hershey has run this small, well-organized store for 16 years all by himself, starting out as a jobber, and later opening up for retail sales. He suggested calling if you come from any distance because he varies his days off, usually taking Monday for himself. He sticks to hardware and groceries, and reduces damaged goods by 25%; "really damaged goods" go for ½ price! Dog food is an especially good buy; he rebags the broken bags of dry dog food and sells it for 15¢/lb.

BARGAINS GALORE

431 N.W. 9th
Hours: M-Sat. 10-6
Handicapped access: yes

222-2185
VISA, MC, checks

Unclaimed and over-age freight fills this warehouse store that has been in Northwest Portland for 20 years, open to the public only for the last 7. Items range from down jackets to tires to slug bait. New Uniroyal and Goodyear tires were 25% off, an Alpine Design down jacket 30% off the day we visited. Manager Geri Pearlman said that often an entire shipment of clothes will be of one size, but we noted a wide selection of both size and style in men's suits (including brands like Botany 500, Cricketeer, and Hart, Shaftener & Marx) at ½ off. Women's Sasson jeans were 50% off, with bargains on other women's apparel.

Kitchenware, hardware, food, skis, carpets, furniture, and some toys were available, but supply and selection depends on what is left on the freight dock. Mrs. Pearlman will call customers looking for something in particular. No cash refunds are made, but exchanges or credit can be arranged on case-by-case basis.

THE BEE COMPANY

800 N. Killingsworth   283-3171
Hours: M-Sat. 9-6   VISA, MC, checks
Handicapped access: yes

Anyone who wants to save money should know about the Bee
Company. Refused, unclaimed, and damaged goods – from linoleum and paint to butter and eggs – are sold in 3 adjacent
stores. Nothing fancy, but grocery prices are discounted a minimum of 20% and most of what we saw was not damaged. Dry
dog food in torn sacks is a good buy. One store has all the hardware, linoleum, and paint at a minimum of 33% off retail.
Another with the furniture, appliances, and carpeting is much
the same. Everything should be checked carefully by the customer because no returns are accepted, but it's definitely worth
a monthly grocery shopping trip or a call when home improve-
ment items are needed.

CITY LIQUIDATORS

830 S.E. 3rd   238-4477
Hours: 8-6, every day   VISA, MC, checks
      except Christmas & Thanksgiving

The large, overstuffed warehouse on the railroad tracks near
the Willamette River is charged with energy, much of it ignited
by the personality of the owner, Walter Pellett, who runs his
operation with a sense of humor and a love of people and merchandising. Furniture is the biggest item – he said he has the
best buys in office furniture in town. When Frederick and Nel-
son bought out the Portland Lipman's store, he got all the old
cash registers; a wig manufacturer went bankrupt, and he got
their 4,600 unsold wigs. Besides the more ordinary surplus
items, he has gotten exotic shipments like a several volume
Chinese library he sold for an elderly man or wool rugs from
Nepal. A visit is as much entertainment as shopping, but we did
find the wooden file box to store the research on this book
there for only 99¢!

DISCOUNT MART

6729 N.E. Killingsworth   no phone
Hours: M-F 9-6:30, Sat. 9:30-6:30   VISA, MC, checks
Handicapped access: yes

This variety store sells a wide range of goods – shampoo, kitchen ware, toiletries, notions – about 20% less than in grocery or drug stores. The items are all new, none damaged – the owner just buys what he can find at lower prices.

THE LIQUIDATOR

12600 S.W. 1st, Bvrt.   **641-0093**
Hours: Th-F 10-5:30; Sat. 10-5   **VISA, MC, checks**
Handicapped access: yes

This well-stocked and carefully-managed liquidator specializes in sportswear and outdoor equipment, although a variety of items (including greeting cards at ½ price) was stocked the day we visited. They are the only outlet in Portland for Columbia Sportswear irregulars and overstocks, which are sold at 10% over the wholesale price – an average savings of 20% to 25% on all garments. Any defect is carefully marked, and a tag explains the difficulty for easy evaluation.

Names in sports equipment available the day we visited included Nike, Spalding, Arai, and the overstocks from Washington Quilt – manufacturer and supplier of sleeping bags to many national retail outlets, including REI – are consistently available at substantial savings. A large variety of sporting goods was available: Sterno, fishing rods and lures, golf balls, racquetball racquets, etc., and hardware items and garden tools were well-stocked. Merchandise does change, however, and a call may save time searching for a specific item. Always stocked and *not* seconds are Swiss Army knives and Mountain Home freeze-dried foods at a 20% discount. Refunds and returns are allowed on all merchandise.

RAILROAD SURPLUS STORE

7920 N.E. Glisan   **no phone**
Hours: T-Sat. 9:30-5   **VISA, MC, checks**
Handicapped access: yes

This tiny liquidator is stocked floor-to-ceiling with food, fabric, notions, children's clothing, picture frames, toys, and greeting cards without envelopes, to name just a few of the plethora of items. Canned goods and other nonperishable grocery items were 15% off, greeting cards 25% off, buttons (on their cards) ½ price. Selling "whatever we can get that fits in the store," the owner relies on distressed goods, closeouts, and bankruptcies for his merchandise. All sales are final.

VARIETY DISCOUNT STORE

3003 S.E. Division   **238-6518**
Hours: M-Sat. 9:30-6, F 9:30-8   **VISA, MC, checks**
Handicapped access: yes

This new, small "discount" store sells salesmen's samples and wholesaler's seconds or damaged goods an average of 25% off the retail price. Stock is varied, but not extensive, and discount merchandise is supplemented by some regularly-priced retail items. The emphasis the day we visited was on kitchen and hardware items, and a recent supply of baby clothes was at 33% less than the manufacturer's suggested price. A call before visiting would help determine in-stock items.

THE VILLAGE STORE

6108 N.E. Glisan   **236-2258**
Hours: M-Sat. 10-5   **VISA, MC, checks**
Handicapped access: two steps

A typical liquidator of damaged freight, the Village Store has an amazing assortment of merchandise from nonperishable groceries to clothing, paperback books, fabrics, and wrapping paper. Paperback books were ½ price, Christmas wrapping paper was 25% less. It's the kind of place to check each time you go by, just to see what the newest bargain is.

Luggage

(Also see Catalog Discounters,
Flea Markets, Thrift Shops)

MEIER & FRANK WAREHOUSE SALE — See Store Outlets

Medical Supplies, Clinics

FAIRWAY OPTICAL

625 S.W. Washington	224-0026
Hours: T-F 10-6, Sat. 10-1	Checks
Handicapped access: yes	
Other locations:	
S.W. 185th & Baseline, Bvrt.	642-5654
8426 S.E. Stark	253-7168

Membership in the Fairway Optical plan is $10, and members may purchase lenses and frames at cost-plus-20%. Single vision lenses and frames begin at $19.95, and the firm advertises that it carries any frame on the market. Lenses are ground to your prescription.

GROUP OPTICAL DISPENSING, INC.

2927 E. Burnside	239-006
Hours: M-F 9-5:30, Sat. 10-2	VISA, MC, checks
Handicapped access: yes	

If you have your prescription and $5 for a 2-year membership fee ($2.75 for those over 65), you can purchase a pair of single vision glasses for $35. Bifocals start at $45, and trifocals at $60. Tints, plastic, and oversize lenses are more expensive, but the company has more than 700 frames to choose from. An optometrist is on duty and will do examinations and prescriptions for a fee. Work is guaranteed and will be replaced if brought in during the first 2 weeks and if analysis shows the glasses to have been defective.

MEDIC PHARMACY, INC.

1016 S.W. Clay	222-9611
Hours: M-F 9-6	Checks
Handicapped access: yes	

This is a pharmacy in the proper sense – no candy bars, toothpaste or paperback books. By carrying only prescriptions and buying in volume when possible, they keep prices down on many drugs, though not on all. A call to them and to your neighborhood pharmacy will let you know if they are worth a trip. On a comparison check, we found Medic to be almost 20% cheaper on 2 often-used medications, but only 25¢-40¢ cheaper on several others. Their biggest volume of sales is through the mail, which carries a 50¢ surcharge.

MT. HOOD COMMUNITY COLLEGE DENTAL CLINIC

26000 S.E. Stark, Gresham   667-6422
Hours: Usually M-F 8-5   Checks
Handicapped access: yes

Tired of paying high prices just to get your teeth cleaned twice a year? The dental hygiene students at the Community College need practice and only charge $5 a sitting. Students and senior citizens can have the same services for only $2. X-rays will be taken and sent to your regular dentist for $7 (full mouth set) and $3 (bite-wing only). A licensed dentist does needed dental work for low income and welfare clients at reduced rates, and prospective patients must register for treatment between January and June for appointments scheduled during the school year.

OREGON RETIRED PERSON'S PHARMACY

1501 S.W. Taylor   226-4141
Hours: M-Sat. 8:30-5   Checks
Handicapped access: yes

Run by the American Association of Retired Persons, the pharmacy offers free mail delivery of prescriptions to anyone over 55 years of age who is a member of the Association. Membership is $4 annually. More exciting, though, is that their drugs are priced well below those of most other pharmacies and are sold to anyone regardless of age. A comparison of several drugs showed more than a 25% savings over most retail outlets.

UNIVERSITY OF OREGON DENTISTRY SCHOOL

611 S.W. Campus Dr.   225-8867
Hours: M-F 9-12, 1-4:30   VISA, MC, checks
Handicapped access: yes

You can save ½ to ⅔ on your dental bills if you don't mind making appointments 3 or 4 months in advance. Teenagers, however, can have immediate appointments because their teeth are at a more critical development stage. Emergency treatment can also be had within 2 days. Dental students do all of the work, with the more complicated jobs done by the more advanced students. A dentist is always in attendance during the work. The school has no billing system, so bills must be paid the day of the service.

Movies

Unless you are a film buff or someone who must talk about the latest movies at every party, you can see almost any film for much less than the standard $4 adult admission by keeping track of the "discount" theaters. Many play the films after the first-runs are over, sometimes only a few months after the film is released, and most charge less than ½ the first-run admission. Those theaters which always advertise low movie prices are listed below, with the adult admission prices we found.

For those who insist on seeing the first run of a movie, it is still possible to save money, and skip the long lines, too. Almost every theater in town has a "bargain hour" – the first hour after the doors open. That means usually until 6 p.m. on weekdays and until 2 p.m. on the weekends. The prices during that hour are ½ or ⅓ the normal prices.

Aloha Theater, 18295 S.W. Tualatin-Valley Hwy., 649-6191, $1.50
Cinema V, 11011 S.E. Main, Milw., 659-3678, $1.25
Clinton St. Theater, 2522 S.E. Clinton, 238-8899, $1.50
Esquire, 838 N.W. 23rd, 222-3477, $1.75
Guild, 829 S.W. 9th, 226-0044, $2.50 (Sr. Citizens $1.50)
Joy, 11595 S.W. Pacific Highway, Tigard, 639-1482, $2.75
KGON Midnight Movie – Fifth Avenue Theater, 510 S.W. Hall, 224-6038, 92¢
Mt. Hood, 401 E. Powell, Gresham, 665-0604, $2
Northgate, 8704 N. Lombard, 286-1768, $2
The Roseway, 7229 N.E. Sandy Blvd., 281-5713, $2.50
Sellwood, 1323 S.E. Tacoma, 234-3254, $2

Paper Goods

GENERAL AMERICAN THEATRE SUPPLY CO.

3202 S.E. Hawthorne Blvd.   **231-7673**
Hours: M-F 8-5   **Checks**
Handicapped access: yes

This bulk food, paper products, and janitorial supply house sells to the public at the same prices it sells to theaters. That means those big candy bars can be had for ½ the price paid at a movie. Candy is sold by case lots of 24 or 48 but will also be sold as units for a bit more than the case price. The store also carries a vast line of Sweetheart and Royal Chinet plates, and hot and cold cups. The case lots of 1,000 or 2,500 can be sold in tubes of 100 or 50. Popped and unpopped popcorn is also available.

PAPER FACTORY OUTLET STORE

13505 S.E. Johnson Rd. (off Oregon 224)   **654-0021**
Hours: M-F 9-5, Sat. 9-4   **VISA, MC, checks**
Handicapped access: yes

All merchandise in this California paper company outlet is priced a minimum of 5% off normal retail prices, and a sliding discount scale is used for an additional discount: 5% for purchases over $25, 7.5% for over $50, and 10% for over $100. The best buys are on factory overruns or seconds, especially of restaurant (2-ply) dinner napkins rejected because of color or pattern inconsistency, toilet paper, paper towels and paper plates, all of which can be purchased in large quantities. An especially attractive saving is on gift wrap and ribbon, which you measure, cut, and roll yourself for a fraction of the price name brands exact. A variety of patterns and colors was available, and Christmas wraps are sold all year long. It is a good idea to bring your own paper tubes and old ribbon spools to make rolling easier.

A large wedding department offers significant savings on specialty paper products and wedding invitations for at-home receptions. Prices on plastic and styrofoam cups should be checked before buying in large quantities, because we found them higher than in some other discounters.

POPPER'S SUPPLY COMPANY

340 S.E. 7th   234-0576
Hours: M-F 8-4:30   Checks
Handicapped access: yes

Popper's price list reads like an introduction to "Basic Carnival," and if you're giving a party, this is the place to go for many of the ingredients. The prices listed are designed for those who usually buy in large (wholesale) quantities, but anyone can purchase and in smaller amounts. The price on less than the list quantities is somewhat higher, though. Incredible savings are available on paper and styrofoam cups and plates; the day we priced paper products, styrofoam cups were ⅓ the cost of the nearest competitor. Special closeouts on paper products happen from time-to-time: 8-oz. paper hot cups with a bicentennial design were selling for 2¢ each. Call for information on specials. Wedding paper supplies are also carried for your comparison shopping before a large reception. And if you can't pop enough corn yourself, this is the place to get it. Popped corn is sold in 4½-lb. bags, with specialty corns (sour cream and onion?!) slightly higher priced. Fifty-lb. bags of unpopped corn are the minimum, with additional savings for buying several at a time. Share with friends, it won't spoil!

Pet Food

(Also see Liquidators)

PRAIRIE MARKET—See Food, Miscellaneous

WAREMART—See Food, Miscellaneous

Photographic Equipment

(Also see Catalog Discounters)

NORTHWEST MOTION PICTURE EQUIPMENT AUCTION AND SALE

1819 N.W. Everett   **223-5335**
Handicapped access: stairs to basement   **Checks**

In November, Northwest Media Project collects film, lenses, cameras, projectors, and sound equipment on consignment and auctions and sells them to raise money. A preview is held in the morning of the chosen Saturday, and bidding begins in the afternoon. Items may be tested during the preview. A master list of the auction items can be obtained from the Project ahead of the sale by calling them. The Northwest Service Center is remodeling to allow easy access to the basement.

Plants

DISCOUNT PLANTS

8775 S.W. Canyon Rd.   No phone
Hours: M-F 11:30-6:30, Sat. 11:30-5:30   Checks
Handicapped access: 4 steps
Other location:
12620 S.W. Main St., Tigard

Some of the cheapest plants in town are in this tiny, crowded store. Though the owners can't stock too many exotics in the small space, they can get you whatever you want from a warehouse in a matter of days. All hanging plants – ferns, spider plants, etc. – were $5 when we visited. The store runs specials when they get big shipments and will let regular customers know through a mailing list.

THE PLANT STOP

2653 N.W. Vaughn   292-8445
Hours: M-F 11-6, Sat. 11-4   Checks
Handicapped access: yes
Other location:
9009 S.W. Canyon Rd.   No phone

Skip the florists, the grocery, and drug stores for your plants. The Plant Stop can get you whatever you need or want (that is, that's legal!) for a lot less. We bought a 2-ft. tall bird's nest fern for $5, ½ the price of a smaller one we saw in a florist's shop. All upright plants in 6" pots were $5, most hanging plants were $7 the day we visited. The store is tiny, but shipments come in weekly, and owner Roger Koepplin said he could order what he didn't have in stock.

RANCHO SELF-SERVICE FLOWERS

8605 S.W. Beaverton-Hillsdale Hwy.   292-6090
Hours: 9-9 every day   VISA, MC, checks
Handicapped access: yes
Other locations:
2010 W. Burnside   227-2950

3575 S.E. Division   232-7204
N.E. 106th & Halsey   256-1144
4607 S.E. Boardman, Milw.   654-5016
599 S.W. "A," Lake Oswego   636-8909

Walk in, find what you want on the tables and rows of
flowers, pick out your bouquet, and take it to the counter.
Though the store will make up bouquets as any other florist
will, the self-service aspect to the flower selling keeps prices
down on the cut flowers. Roses were $1 each or $6.98 to
$7.98/dozen; short-stemmed, $3.98/dozen. Plants were not
quite as cheap as those in the discount plant stores we visited,
but still lower than at some florist shops. No refunds or credits
are given, but exchanges will be made.

Pottery

CLAY WORKS POTTERY

3125 E. Burnside   232-0320
Hours: M-F 11-7, Sat. 11-5   VISA, MC, checks
Handicapped access: 5 steps to 2nd floor

Like all craftsmen, potters sometimes make mistakes. If the mistakes aren't too bad, like poor glazing on a flower pot or a crack where it won't be seen, the work is still salable. Clay Works usually has a few seconds marked down according to the severity of the flaw. A planter with a glazing design flaw was marked down ⅓ the day we shopped. One with a crack across the bottom (necessitating another saucer to catch the water) was marked less than ½ price.

RETAIL POTTERY OUTLET

4069 N.E. Union   282-1135
Hours: M-Sat. 8:30-5   VISA, MC, checks
Handicapped access: yes

There is nothing fancy in this warehouse for ceramic planters, but if a standard clay or colored pot is needed, prices are lower here than at the supermarket or nursery. Check over the merchandise because some may be cracked and still in the first quality areas. Retail prices are kept between 20%-40% over wholesale, and 10% can be saved by buying a case of clay pots. One side of the room holds the damaged pots – some which have unnoticeable blemishes for some savings.

Records and Stereo Equipment

(Also see Auctions, Catalog Discounters)

BIRD'S SUITE RECORDS

3736 S.E. Hawthorne   235-6224
Hours: M-Sat. 11-6   VISA, MC, checks
Handicapped access: yes

Consignments are welcome at this jam-packed record store which stocks about 6,000 albums of jazz, rock and roll, blues and some classical music. The store keeps 25% of the sale price. Used records in perfect condition sell for ½ the usual retail price; sealed records run about $1 more. An out-of-print record can run as high as a new one, even if considerably used. Records traded for others garner about 20% more in merchandise than if sold for cash. Check the box of 50¢ and 99¢ records – it could contain a collector's gem or a bit of nostalgia. The manager will play records before you buy them, and records can be exchanged if found defective, but no refunds are given.

DJANGO

1111 S.W. Stark   227-4381
Hours: M-F 10-9, Sat. 10-6,   VISA, MC, checks
        Sun. 12-6
Handicapped access: yes

Oregon's first and largest used record store, Django is the most organized of those we visited. Each rock, western, jazz, and blues star is indexed alphabetically, as well as are classical composers. The store, which now stocks 15,000 albums, started out as an outlet for jazz collectors and traders, but the rock market, needing an outlet, flooded the store. Rock sales now enable the store to cater to out-of-print record collecting. Records traded for other records get 10% more in value than selling for cash. Defective records must be returned within 5 days.

GALAXY RECORDS AND TAPES

3768 S.E. Hawthorne   **231-1468**
Hours: M-Sat. 12-10, Sun. 1-5   **VISA, MC, checks**
Handicapped access: yes

This small store concentrates on country and rock albums, with a few comedy and classical records on the racks – 8 total the day we visited. All new albums sold for about $1 less than regular retail. Used records were in one bin and unorganized, all for under $2. Quite a few old 45s were also available at low prices.

GREAT AMERICAN STEREO WAREHOUSE

N.W. Couch & 1st   **223-3193**
Hours: M-F 10-9, Sat. 10-6, Sun. 12-5   **VISA, MC, checks**
Handicapped access: 5 steps*
Other locations:
13755 S.E. McLoughlin, Milw.   **653-1155**
8614 S.W. Hall, Bvrt.   **646-6882**

You won't find chrome and glass display shelves or plush sound rooms here, but low overhead and volume buying for the 3 Portland-area and 2 Seattle stores helps to keep down prices on 29 major brands of stereo equipment. Ads in Thursday and Sunday papers will give you the best idea of their prices. Striving to stay below all competitors, the store has prices usually 10%-20% below their major counterparts. And, although the salespeople won't quote prices over the phone, they will tell a purchaser if they can beat a price found somewhere else. Cash refunds are available up to 7 days from purchase, and equipment can be traded in on better equipment during the first 30 days of ownership. Financing is available, and the store will handle servicing, even providing a loan of similar equipment for the time yours is in the shop.

*Note, parking and access are easier at the other two locations.

PARK AVENUE RECORDS

832 S.W. Park   222-4773
Hours: M-Sat. 11-6, Sun. 12-5   Cash only
Handicapped access: yes

Any used record over $2 should be as good as new, according to the manager, and the store will take back defective records and tapes. The store stocks mostly rock, with some pop, blues, classical, and a few imports. Tapes are a good buy (if you can find good ones) because they are sold at record prices and are usually 33% lower than retail tape prices.

YESTERDAY RECORDS

3822 N.E. Sandy Blvd.   287-3610
Hours: T-F 12:30-6:30, Sat. 10:30-5:30   VISA, MC, checks
Handicapped access: yes

The biggest selection of used 45s in town is here, and owner Bob Gallucci keeps a wide selection of music in his inventory usually of 11,000 albums. All used, in-print records sold for $2.95 (double albums for $3.95), regardless of what the new price would be. Gallucci also maintains an "easy listening" section, which most other stores ignore. Collectors looking for out-of-print records often shop here, too. Gallucci buys and trades used records and will take back defective records, but he carefully examines all sales before they leave the store.

Sporting Goods

(Also see Catalog Discounters,
Liquidators, Thrift Stores)

General

ANDY AND BAX

324 S.E. Grand   234-7538
Hours: M-Th, Sat. 9-6, F 9-9   VISA, MC, checks
Handicapped access: yes

Andy and Bax has been around since World War II, starting
out as solely an Army surplus outlet and later branching into
general sporting goods. Now, any outdoors enthusiast will
direct you to this huge store for bargains in military surplus
clothing and equipment that serves today's leisure activities of
camping, hiking, and skiing. Wool glove liners, canvas gloves,
the famous 13-button Navy pants, paratrooper pants with tight
ankles and lots of pockets are popular. Army artillary bags
have all kinds of uses from funky purses to fishing creels to
small day packs. All are priced at what the market will bear
and usually much lower than what similar "sporting goods" sell
for. A 2-oz. can of Army sun screen was an extraordinary buy
the day we visited. Some of the sizes are a bit bizarre, and
clothing should be examined carefully for fit and flaws. (For ex-
ample, Japanese military fatigues have what we would con-
sider to be *very* short legs!) However, hems and seams are
usually wide, and a little time at the sewing machine can work
wonders. Refunds on returned merchandise are available if a
garment just cannot be altered to fit once examined at home.

DANNER SHOE MFG. CO. — See Clothing

MEIER & FRANK WAREHOUSE SALE — See Store
Outlets

PRO GOLF DISCOUNT DISTRIBUTORS, INC.

5253 N.E. Sandy Blvd.   **282-5282**
Hours: M-Th 10-6, F 10-8, Sat. 10-5   **VISA, MC, checks**
Handicapped access: yes

Parker and Rawlings gloves, MacGregor and Ram clubs and balls, Coleman jackets can all be found at a discount at this professional-status golf store. Top-flight equipment is sold here, and the manager knows golf and sells the same equipment with the same expertise found in pro shops. With 50 stores around the country, Pro Golf can afford to buy in volume and at lower prices. Clubs are generally 20%-50% off list price, shoes 15%-30%. They also handle closeouts, which can save as much as 50% less than list prices.

REI CO-OP

1798 Jantzen Beach Center   **283-1300**
Hours: M, T, Sat. 9:30-6; W-F 9:30-9   **VISA, MC, checks**
Handicapped access: yes

Climbing, hiking, skiing, trekking, whatever you want to do outdoors, REI has the clothes and equipment. Prices aren't discounted, but co-op members who pay a one-time-only $2 membership fee get a dividend at the end of the year based on the amount of money they spent. Though the amount returned varies as to the co-op profits, dividends have hovered around 10%. A mail order catalog lists 2,200 items, and the store has many more. The fall and spring sales are the best time to purchase expensive items, but it is wise to join the people camped in line overnight to get the best selection. Entire shelves of clothing have been known to disappear in a matter of minutes. The catalog lists sale dates. Rental equipment is also available. Refunds or exchanges will be made.

Ski Equipment, Clothing

ALPHA KAPPA PSI SKI SALE

PSU — Smith Memorial Center   **229-4580**
Hours: call beforehand   **VISA, MC, checks**
Handicapped access: yes

The professional and business fraternity has held an annual

sale since 1970 of new and used ski equipment, usually during 2 days in November. Both the used (consigned) and new equipment from area shops are on sale with savings of up to 50%. The whole range of downhill and cross-country skis, boots, poles, and clothing can be found. The fraternity keeps 15% of the consigned price, but consignors are allowed to set their own prices.

CASCADDEN'S SKI RESALE

1533 N.W. 24th   **222-5662**
Hours: T-F 11-6, Sat. 11-4   **VISA, MC, checks**
Handicapped access: yes

Ice and roller skates and hiking boots are sold along with skis, boots, poles, and some clothing at this family-run consignment store. Open from October to March, the store will accept most sporting goods, except for old leather, lace ski boots, for a 25% cut on the sale. Most items are priced below 50% of the original price. No returns are accepted.

MOGUL MOUSE SKI SHOPS SKI-GRAB

Multnomah County Exposition Center   **1-272-3391**
Hours: F-Sun. 10-5   **VISA, MC, checks**
2060 N.E. Marine Dr.
Handicapped access: yes

This 3-day sale the last weekend in October pulls together the inventories of the Mogul Mouse Ski Shops in Government Camp, Eugene, and Springfield for savings of up to 70%. Last year's rentals, demonstration models, and clothing are the best bargains. The tennis equipment stocked in the summer is also cleared at this time – clothing 50% off, shoes up to 70% off, racquets 40% off. Head, K2, Hart, Kastle, Dynastar ski equipment are all available along with other well-known brands. All sales are final, no phone or mail orders are accepted, and no layaways are kept.

MOUNTAIN SHOP SNIAGRAB SALE

628 N.E. Broadway   **288-6768**
Hours: Th-F 10-9, Sat. 10-6   **VISA, MC, checks**
Handicapped access: yes

The Mountain Shop's Sniagrab (get what that is spelled backwards?) Sale began in 1958 and still offers great ski bargains the final week in September. Savings from 10%-50% are available on both new and last year's models of name brands like Nordica, Heierling, Hexcel, Olin, and Salomon. Cross-country and downhill equipment and clothing are included in the sale. Sizes are somewhat limited on last year's models.

OSBORN AND ULLAND, INC. SNIAGRAB

1302 Lloyd Center   **288-7396**
Hours: F 12-10, Sat. 10-8   **VISA, MC, checks**
Handicapped access: yes

The Mountain Shop may claim it was the first to name its big fall sale by spelling "bargains" backwards, but Osborn and Ulland had had the sale long before in Seattle, finally bringing it to their Portland store. The 2-day sale in September is heavily advertised in the sports sections of local newspapers. The biggest savings are on last-year's and discontinued models of boots, skis, and clothing (both downhill and cross-country) which are liquidated to make way for the new styles. Prices are from 30%-60% off the new retail prices. All sales are final; no layaway, phone, or mail orders are accepted. Availability is limited to stock on hand, and not all sizes are available in all models.

SCHNEE VOGELI SKI SALE

628 N.E. Broadway (at the Mountain Shop)   **288-6768**
Hours: M-F 10-9, Sat. 10-6, Sun. 12-5   **VISA, MC, checks**
Handicapped access: yes

The Schnee Vogeli Ski Club holds a 3-day sale in October of each year to raise money. Consignment items are accepted, with 20% of the selling price going to the club. We bought a pair of downhill skis and boots there – skis for $20 and boots for $60. All sales are final, but if you find you don't like what you have bought, you can take them down and resell them yourself.

SKI EXCHANGE

212 S.W. Salmon   **223-0249**
Hours: M-Sat. 11-6:30   **VISA, MC, checks**
Handicapped access: yes

Only equipment and clothing less than 4 years old is accepted for consignment and is marked 50% or more below the original cost. Both downhill and cross-country boots, skis, poles, and clothing are available in men's, women's, and children's sizes. Also sold are several ski areas' last year's rental equipment, offering a wide variety of sizes in relatively inexpensive but usually trustworthy brands. New equipment for children is stocked, and an exchange system has been established whereby outgrown equipment can be traded for a percentage of the cost of a larger size. The trade-ins are then sold as used. The store is open from October to March. No returns are accepted.

SPORTIQUE WEST

4804 S.W. 77th, Bvrt.   **292-3567**
Hours: M-F 11-9, Sat. 10-6   **VISA, MC, checks**
Handicapped access: down stairs

Open from September to May, this basement store in the Raleigh Hills Shopping Center is the outlet for the Ski Chalet's last year's clothes and beginner's equipment. Eidelweis, White Stag, Nordica, Serac, and First Down brands are among those sold. Best buys are found on last year's merchandise which is priced at ½ the original price. The store also handles the closeouts and bankruptcy stocks of other outlets. Men's and women's clothes are available, but children's wear is sparse. Credit is given on returns, full refunds on first-run merchandise. A sale at the end of the year offers greater savings.

Store Outlets

MEIER AND FRANK WAREHOUSE SALE

Corner of N.W. 14 & Irving   **227-4400**
Hours: call; they vary from   **Checks, M&F credit card**
    year-to-year
Handicapped access: 3 steps

Once a year, usually in October, Portland's largest department store hauls its floor samples, slow sellers, broken sets, and torn packages to its warehouse, piles them on tables, cuts the prices drastically, and opens the doors Friday night, Saturday, and Sunday afternoons. It's a crowded affair but worth the time spent browsing. Poly-fill comforters were ½ off, as were Samsonite luggage and special ordered draperies (which had been returned) the day we visited. Farberware open stock cookware was 33% off, perfect for filling in a starter set. A cartload of all kinds of saucers which had lost their cups were selling for a penny each – "perfect for trap or skeet shooting" the sign read! We bought 6 for putting under potted plants.

MONTGOMERY WARD WAREHOUSE SALE ROOM

5905 N. Marine Dr.   **286-4509**
Hours: M-Sat. 10-6   **Checks, Ward's credit card**
Handicapped access: yes

A store's delivery men are often its worst enemy, and the bumps, scratches, and dents that result from delivery accidents put many items in the bargain bins. Montgomery Ward's warehouse is full of furniture, refrigerators, stoves, televisions, and stereos that have some external damage. The amount of damage sets the percentage of markdown, but they advertise savings of up to 75%. The price does not include a warranty, but a repair policy can be purchased, still keeping cost under the retail price. Returns can be negotiated; delivery is available for a set charge.

Take the Rivergate/T-6/Marine Dr. W. exit off I-5 N, and follow the signs towards Kelly Point Park and T-6 to the warehouse.

SEARS RETAIL OUTLET STORE

5230 N. Basin   **238-2398**
Hours: M-Sat. 9:30-5:30   **Sears credit card, checks**
Handicapped access: yes

Freight-damaged and discontinued merchandise, customer returns, and floor samples from the Sears stores in the area are collected here and sold at discounts depending on the condition of each item. Anything that appears in a Sears catalog can appear in the store, from tractor lawnmowers to mirrors, furniture, bedding, and clothing. They advertise that customer satisfaction is guaranteed, and all usual warranties apply.

SEARS SURPLUS STORE

718 N.E. Grand   **238-2080**
Hours: M-F 9:30-9, Sat. 9:30-5:30,   **Sears credit card,**
**   Sun. 12-5**   **checks**
Handicapped access: yes

This is a great place to look for drapes, storm windows, or screens. The custom-made designs that have been returned by dissatisfied customers are marked down substantially – ½ price for windows and screens, $12.88 for any size storm window when we visited. First quality discontinued merchandise carries the same "satisfaction guaranteed" warranty that catalog merchandise carries. Clothing, sewing patterns, calculators, small appliances, kitchen cabinets, suitcases, and zippers were all in the surplus store when we visited. Large items will be delivered, but the trucks do not run every day.

SMITH'S BUDGET CENTER

3103 S.E. Division   **234-9351**
Hours: T-F 9-9, Sat. 9-6   **VISA, MC, checks**
Handicapped access: yes

Across the street from Smith's Home Furnishings is the store that sells the "scratch and dent specials." Discontinued, one-of-a-kind and damaged goods are sold here at least 10%-15% less than across the street. Some returned merchandise is also sold here. We found microwave ovens marked down $70. All warranties are good, and the store will deliver for a fee.

Thrift Shops

ALL AMERICAN THRIFT STORE

2080 S.E. Oak Grove Blvd., Milw.   653-6453
Hours: T-Sat. 10-3   Checks
Handicapped access: curb

Sponsored by the Clackamas County Association for Retarded Citizens and the Kiwanis Club of North Clackamas County, the thrift shop accepts donated items for sale. The bulk of the goods are clothing, and books with some small household goods for sale.

ASSISTANCE LEAGUE THRIFT SHOP

735 N.W. 23rd   227-7093
Hours: M-F 10:30-3:30, Sat. 10:30-3   Checks
Handicapped access: yes

The money raised in this small thrift shop supports the Creston School Dental Clinic. Both men's and women's clothing are very conservatively priced, about 10% of retail. Check the Signature Rack near the door for the better designer labels. A dressing room is available, and all sales are final.

BARGAIN TREE

837 S.W. 3rd   227-7413
Hours: M-F 10-5, Sat. 11-4   VISA, MC, checks
Handicapped access: yes

The Junior League-run resale shop is the biggest in town of its kind. All goods are donated by Junior League members and priced at thrift shop rates. Designer fashions are marked with orange tags. Certain tables hold items that haven't sold and are finally given away to whomever thinks they can use them. Half-off days are held the 3rd day of each month, followed by "bag sales" of the leftover items: all the clothing that fits in one large shopping bag can be bought for $3. Sales are held the 1st Monday in December for Christmas, 2 weeks before Easter, and in September just before school starts. Some furniture is consigned, and a few houseware items are sold. All sales are final, but items can be held for one week. A mailing list notifies customers of seasonal sales and specials.

BLUEJAY WEARHAUS

6418 S.E. Foster Road   **774-2601**
Hours: T-Sat. 10-5   **Checks**
Handicapped access: yes

Only small items are sold at this thrift shop which supports the Lutheran High School. Though clothes are in the majority, the store also carries some appliances, new greeting cards without envelopes (great for decoupage at a penny a piece), books, and some sporting goods. A ½ price sale is held in the fall.

CHRISTIE'S ATTIC THRIFT SHOP

7907 S.E. 13th   **236-0222**
Hours: T-F 9:30-4, Sat. 10-3   **Checks**
Handicapped access: yes

The money from this small thrift shop in the Sellwood antique district goes to the Christie School for emotionally disturbed girls. Lots of children's clothing is available – all utilitarian but cheap. A set of Encyclopedia Brittanica was priced at $20 when we visited, and *National Geographics* were 15¢ each. Half price sales are held in the spring and fall to make way for seasonal clothes. Moreover, each Friday a different item is put on sale for ½ price. Donated items are accepted, but the store will not pick up or deliver.

THE CHURCH MOUSE THRIFT SHOP

1422 S.W. 11th   **222-2031**
Hours: T-Sat. 11-3   **VISA, MC, checks**
Handicapped access: several stairs

This small, cluttered thrift shop run by and in The Old Church, would make it easier for shoppers if the salespersons would organize the items better. Clothes prices were very low – those that were marked. Dressing rooms are available, as is layaway. If you don't mind digging through boxes of miscellaneous items, you might find a real bargain.

THE CHURCH OF JESUS CHRIST OF LATTER DAY SAINTS THRIFT SHOP

10330 S.E. 82nd	777-3895
Hours: M 10-5:30, T-Sat. 10-8	Checks
Handicapped access: curb	

A part of the church's Deseret Industries, the store sells the usual donated items – clothing, books, small kitchen appliances – to raise money for the church.

THE CORNER THRIFT SHOP

6258 S.E. Foster Rd.	771-5816
Hours: M-Sat. 12-6	Cash only
Handicapped access: yes	
Other location:	
5241 S.E. 72nd	777-8106

The Foster Road store carries mostly small items – used records, paperback books, old *Playboys* and cartridge tapes. The S.E. 72nd Avenue store carries larger items, including furniture and appliances. The store will pick up donated goods and is affiliated with the Oregon Epilepsy Association.

COUNCIL THRIFT SHOP

300 S.W. Stark	227-2877
Hours: M-F 9:30-5, Sat. 9:30-4	Checks
Handicapped access: 1 step	

Run by the Portland branch of the National Council of Jewish Women, the Council Thrift Shops sells mostly clothing – men's, women's, and a good stock of children's – at very low prices. A brand new pair of Nina patent leather women's shoes was marked at $7 the day we visited. They also carry odds and ends of kitchen utensils and home decorating items, though nothing very large. All sales are final.

GOODWILL INDUSTRIES OF OREGON STORES

1925 S.E. 6th	238-6165
Hours: M-Sat. 9-5:30	VISA, MC, checks
Handicapped access: yes	
Other locations:	
9130 S.E. Woodstock	774-7503

8641 N. Lombard	286-5646
5270 N.E. Union	281-7323
4100 S.W. Griffith Rd.	643-6099

Although Goodwill has been easing out of the large appliance and "hard to repair" market, and has stopped picking up donated items from homes, it still fills 5 stores and provides some extras that make a visit worthwhile and fun. One of those extras is the "Auxiliary Cottage" where items are handmade or repaired by the women of the Auxiliary and sell for very reasonable prices. The day we visited, placemats, linens, aprons, macrame, and quilts were well stocked and some very finely done. In a "Collector's Corner", we found a flute for $65 – in good condition and with all its pads. Back issues of magazines were selling for ½ the new price.

According to the manager, Goodwill is allowed to sell up to 10% of its total merchandise new, and still maintain its non-profit status. This allows the store to always have some seasonal items on hand, giving the shopper a more comprehensive selection of merchandise. Sometimes the prices at Goodwill are beat by retailer's "loss leader" items, but most new and used items sell at less to considerably less than normal retail. Especially good buys were noticed on crochet threads, a tuxedo, White Stag remnants, and paperback books.

NEARLY NEW SHOP

3415 S.E. Hawthorne	235-8053
Hours: M-Sat. 10-5	Cash only
Handicapped access: yes	

Run by the Portland Chapter of the Hadassah, all proceeds from sales go to supporting the Hadassah Hebrew University Medical Center in Israel, a picture of which is displayed over the cashier's stand. Clothing predominates here, with polyesters reigning supreme. Although the store has nowhere near everything, it did have the proverbial kitchen sink on the day we visited, some kitchen utensils, paperback books, and a few drapes. A good selection of used uniforms was available – all white and pretty short.

PARRY CENTER THRIFT STORE

709 N.W. 23rd	227-6201

Hours: M-F 10-4, Sat. 11-3   **Checks**
Handicapped access: yes

Children's clothing is well priced here, almost everything being under $1. Men's and women's clothing is also available, as are the usual kitchen odds and ends. Having no truck to pick up items, the store does not carry appliances or furniture. The profits support the Parry Center for Children, which is a resident treatment center for the emotionally disturbed. The available dressing room is very necessary since clothes are not sized. All sales are final.

PHILO HOUSE

4611 S.E. Hawthorne   **232-3992**
Hours: M-Sat. 10-3   **Checks**
Handicapped access: yes

Run by the Holy Trinity Greek Orthodox Church, this tiny shop carries mostly donated clothing items.

RED, WHITE, AND BLUE THRIFT STORE

19239 S.E. McLoughlin Blvd.   **655-3444**
Hours: M-Sat. 9-6   **Checks**
Handicapped access: curb

The usual range of thrift store merchandise, with emphasis on used clothing, is tidily arranged in a clean, organized manner here. Clothes are color and size assembled, and some very nice infants garments were available the day we visited. Dressing rooms are provided, as well as full-length mirrors, but the signs requested buyers to bring their own paper bags. A pair of men's insulated boots in good condition was $5.95; women's jeans from 95¢ to $1.45; hairpieces were $1.95. No refunds or exchanges are permitted, and large items are sold without warranty or delivery.

SALVATION ARMY THRIFT STORE

200 S.E. Union   **235-7806**
Hours: M-Sat. 9-5   **VISA, MC, checks**
Handicapped access: yes
Other locations:
9038 S.E. Foster Rd.   **775-3207**
8836 N. Lombard   **286-9571**

Though not as large as Goodwill Industries, the Salvation Army stores are as clean and as well-organized, with the usual array of castoffs from clothing to couches. The Union Avenue store is a good source of florist's vases for those who haven't collected a personal stock. They provide an inexpensive way to give homegrown or wild bouquets to friends. Furniture and mattresses are reupholstered in the store's workshops. Suitcases sell for about 10% of the retail price. Sewing patterns, though some are a bit dated, are also good buys. Large items costing more than $25 are delivered free to Portland addresses, and senior citizens get a 10% discount on all merchandise.

SOCIETY OF ST. VINCENT DE PAUL STORES

2740 S.E. Powell	234-0598
Hours: M, F 9-8; T-Th, Sat. 9-5,	VISA, MC, checks
Sun. 11-5	
Handicapped access: yes	
Other locations:	
1016 S.W. 3rd	222-4884
740 N. Killingsworth	285-0795
S.E. 32nd & Harrison, Milw.	654-5220
700 Molalla, Oregon City	655-6927

St. Vincent de Paul offers a 30-day warranty on appliances they refurbish, and delivery is free to any Portland address. An "As-is" store is located at the S.E. Powell site, where broken and scratched items and odds and ends can be found for almost nothing. Dickering can be done there, but prices in the rest of the store are set. The Powell store also has an "Antique Boutique." When we visited it was mostly full of older "junque," although a watchful eye and frequent visits might turn up something worthwhile. A fireplace screen for $12 was the best buy when we visited.

THIS OLD HOUSE THRIFT SHOP

3247 N.E. Broadway	284-4322
Hours: T-Sat. 10-4	VISA, MC, checks
Handicapped access: many stairs	

The American Cancer Society has hopped on the bandwagon of money-raising projects, opening a thrift shop in an old 2-story house. Nora Janik also started it to help the low-income people in the area. She keeps a card file for those looking for something special – a crib, perhaps, or a dining table – and allows that person right of first refusal when the item comes in. The first Saturday of each month is a 4-for-1 sale – buy 4 items for the price of the costliest. Paperback books are all ½ the new price. Cancer patients who are losing weight quickly can get free clothing if they have been referred by a doctor.

UNION GOSPEL MISSION THRIFT STORE

5615 S.E. 82nd	**771-3510**
Hours: M-Sat. 9-9	**VISA, MC, checks**
Handicapped access: yes	
Other location:	
11611 S.W. Pacific Hwy., Tigard	**639-6487**

This full-line thrift store had a wide selection and seemingly good prices, although merchandise was not of top quality. Some shirts had holes in them, and a close look should be in order when buying. Cribs, children's clothing, and toys were in good supply and are excellent buys if you are able to do some minor repairs. Used golf balls, bundled in dozen lots, were selling very cheaply. A nice display of somewhat overpriced antiques was shown in one corner of the store. Occasional blue tag specials list all clothing at ½ price, and the stores will provide a truck for pick-up or delivery of larger items, although a fee as much as $15 was charged for a Beaverton delivery. Layaways will be held for 3 days only, and all items are sold as is – no exchanges or refunds.

VALUE VILLAGE THRIFT STORE

5050 S.E. 82nd	**771-5472**
Hours: M-Sat. 9-9, Sun. 10-6	**VISA, MC, checks**
Handicapped access: yes	

Sundays are a good time to shop here because used items are all 20% off. Senior citizens get another 20% off at any time. The store is dusty, so don't wear new clothes if you intend to look through stacks of old *National Geographics* or record albums. They did have a wide selection of new kitchen wares, which were priced somewhat lower than could be found in most retail outlets. They also stocked some new furniture, which was very modest in quality and not discounted much more than other low-cost furniture stores.

VETERANS THRIFT CENTER

12415 S.E. Powell	760-1676
Hours: M-Sat. 9-9, Sun. 11-6	VISA, MC, checks
Handicapped access: yes	
Other location:	
7720 S.E. 82nd	775-4343

Clothing is arranged by color in this thrift store which sells a wide range of donated items from old furniture to sewing patterns and books. All sales are final, but the store will repair or replace a faulty appliance within 15 days. Layaway is available.

VOLUNTEERS OF AMERICA THRIFT STORES

525 S.E. Pine	233-4981
Hours: M-Sat. 9-4:45	Checks
Handicapped access: yes	
Other locations:	
9217 S.E. Foster Rd.	774-3516
919 7th, Oregon City	655-4484
815 N. Lombard	283-2326

Umbrellas for 50¢ were the best bargain when we visited. The Thrift Store also carries some appliances, furniture, odds and ends, and a lot of clothes and shoes. Prices are not marked, and items must be brought to the sales counter to be priced, which makes browsing difficult. A 30-day warranty is put on some appliances, but it is not a general policy, so ask before buying. Delivery carries a charge of $5. For those who sew, we found a good supply of lace from old curtains, tablecloths, and clothing hidden away behind one counter.

WILLIAM TEMPLE THRIFT SHOP

706 N.W. 23rd	222-3328
Hours: M-Sat. 10-4	Checks
Handicapped access: yes	

While most thrift stores price goods according to the quality of the merchandise, this shop has simplified pricing to the basics: all women's dresses are one price (75¢ the day we visited), all men's cotten shirts another, all men's knit shirts yet another. A good search through the racks could turn up some excellent buys. Run by the William Temple House, an Episcopal service organization, the shop carries some larger items, appliances, and furniture, but the emphasis is on clothing. All sales are final.

Toys and Games

(Also see Catalog Discounters)

MEIER & FRANK WAREHOUSE SALE — See Store Outlets

TOY BOX

Hours: Nov. 1-Dec. 24, 10-9 every day   VISA, MC, checks

Because this store is open only during the Christmas season, it is located each year in the cheapest space available, hence its non-address. However, before opening each year, the owner advertises heavily in local newspapers, and a call to Directory Assistance for their phone number can also lead you to them. Ask to get on their mailing list for the easiest trail to their next-year's location.

Calling itself "the ugly store with beautiful prices", it handles discontinued lines, overstocks, samples, and closeouts on toys, Christmas wrap and ribbon, hobbies, novelties, and a few other gift items. Almost everything is marked ½ off the list or suggested prices. Boxes of items are piled on the floor and new ones arrive daily. There are no frills, no returns, no rainchecks, and advertised items are subject to prior sale.

TOY LENDING LIBRARY

1087 S.E. 7th, West Linn   657-4410
Hours: M-F 9-5, 9-9 first Wed. of each month
Handicapped access: curb

The Clackamas County Children's Commission keeps a room stocked with developmental, educational, and just plain fun toys for the children of Clackamas County residents. A $5 annual fee covers a library card on which 3 toys a month can be checked out. The library works in conjunction with the county library bookmobile service which circulates the toys to the outlying areas of the county.

INDEX

Alphabetical

Geographical

Beaverton

Northwest Portland

Oregon City/West Linn

Southeast Portland

Southwest Portland